CAMILLA CHAND

KETO CHAFFLE WORLD
cookbook

QUICK & EASY KETOGENIC WAFFLE RECIPES
FOR DELICIOUS TREATS IN YOUR
LOW-CARB DIET

TABLE OF CONTENTS

INTRODUCTION

ABOUT THIS BOOK..

Welcome to the World of Chaffles! If you're new to the chaffle world this book you like delicious food and quality recipes, this book is going to be a real treat. A chaffle is like a waffle, but much healthier, more versatile and delicious.

If you've always liked waffles but your diet ethic does not allow you to binge on them, discovering chaffles is going to feel like a walk through your favorite amusement park. And if you already know how great chaffles are you know what you're in for. I've always worked in a bakery since I was a little girl, and I think chaffles are one of the best thing that has happened to cooking in the last decade. They're quick to prepare, irresistible and affordable!

in this book you will find many recipes to prepare a great variety of chaffles, sweet and savory, that you can enjoy at breakfast, lunch, dinner or just for a snack! The new chaffle trend is so popular because of their versatility: the limit is really your imagination. The recipes you'll see in this book are the ones that I've found to be my favorites. Welcome to the hottest Keto craze, welcome to Keto Chaffle World!your imagination.

CHAPTER I / WHAT IS A CHAFFLE?

People who are following a Keto diet or simply enjoy eating ketogenic meals will love chaffles, this meal will definitely change their food routine. So, what are chaffles precisely and why all the fuss abut them? They are in fact waffles, but made with cheese which is exactly from where their name derives. Cheese + Waffle = Chaffle.

The crucial difference from well known waffles lays in their composition, instead of a flour based batter, a basic chaffle can be made with just two ingredients, cheese and eggs. Before you ask, yes, no carbs, just a good amount of protein and fats which makes this dish a perfect fit for any ketogenic dietary regimen. Regular waffles provides an unnecessary and undesired amount of carbs for those on a diet and are not recommended for people who are trying to loose weight. The good news is, you won't even notice the difference between the two since chaffles are extremely delicious. You can

have them sweet, savoury, vegetarian, with meat... there are plenty of alternatives so that you'll never run out of options. Some chaffle variations also avoid cheese and are almond flour or coconut flour based. These fantastic food started as a trend among those on restrictive diets. Nonetheless, chaffles have become incredibly popular right now. They are so widely known, that even people who are not on a ketogenic diet wish to give them a try. There are plenty of food combos that are available for you to make, many unique ways to customize chaffles. For all the pizza lovers out there, you can make a delicious pizza chaffle or a chocolate chip chaffles if you want to treat yourself. You may want to layer chaffles and frosting to create your own chaffles tower. There are endless choices. They are amazing for people who are on a ketogenic diet but still want to have waffles in their meal plan. You can have them for breakfast, as a snack or for dessert. As we mentioned before, because of their basic ingredients, chaffles provide a lot of protein that is why they are so filling. Feeling full for a long time means avoid overeating.

THE CHAFFLE MAKER

You are going to require a special machine to shape them amd cook them - the chaffle maker, also called chaffle iron. There are many different brands available on the market, you can find them at your local kitchen equipment store or online. They come with a variety of browning settings, multiple cooking times, non-stick options, and many more features. Most of them are small enough to even tuck into your kitchen drawer. If you already have a waffle maker, it will work just fine even if there are, there are certain differences between these two machines.

CAN THE EGGY FLAVOR BE REPLACED?

Eggs are the main ingredient of chaffles, and this flavour is quite distinctive. Using a strong flavoured cheese will help you limit the eggy taste. Also try to add lime, lemon zest, or orange juice. If you choose to add coconut flour, eggs will definitely be less prevalent. I also included many recipes in this books where I use vanilla drops to sweeten them up. The more ingredients you add, the less likely you'll taste the eggs. Vegetables are great, you can change completely the flavours without adding extra calories! In savoury chaffles you also may try to use truffle to add extra flavour.

CAN I FREEZE MY CHAFFLES?

Yes, you can store them in a freezer for up to 3-4 days. Just place them in a freezer bag with a strip of parchment paper between each one. Don't keep more than two in each bag. You can reheat them in a toaster oven, frying pan, in the microwave or conventional oven before you eat them.

CHAPTER 2 / WHAT IS KETOSIS?

Ketosis is a metabolic state in which your organism utilizes ketones and fats instead of sugar as its primary fuel source. Glucose is stored in the liver and released only when needed for energy. If carbs intakes keep lowering for few days these sugar stores are depleted. Your liver can gain some of the sugar from the amino acids in the proteins you eat. These sugars are not enough to satisfy the needs of your body which is constantly requiring a fuel source.

THE KETOGENIC DIET AND ITS BENEFITS

The ketogenic diet (most commonly called Keto diet) is dietary regimen which promotes the consumption of low-carb and high-fat foods. These selected foods will mostly feed our organism with healthy fats and protein. The caloric intake of our diet will mainly come from fat (70%), protein (20%) and only 10% from carbohydrates. Its is not about calories restriction but rather, foods restriction. As we all know, the human body processes carbs into glucose to generate energy. What maybe we don't hear quite often is that fats, can also be used to generate energy. By ignoring our fats intake we tend to deposit them and that's what makes us overweight. During the keto diet we limit carbs so that the body has to make use of fats in order to produce the energy required by our body. Therefore, ketogenic diet is said to be very highly effective for weight loss. Another crucial point is that when you eat less carbs, the insulin level in the system drops, which means there is less glucose. This particular diet is not just about weight loss but it has many benefits. It improves the level of healthy HDL cholesterol and decreases unhealthy LDL cholesterol. This may reduce the risk of heart diseases. By limiting carbs, we lower the levels of sugar in our blood which also decreases our insulin level. By stabilising insulin levels we increase our energy. Also, a low-carb, high protein and fat diet make our brains more efficient. It can prevent cognitive diseases and control the negative effects of too much inflammation. A low carbs diet helps with digestion and acid reflux and might also increase longevity according to many studies.

FOODS ALLOWED AND NOT ALLOWED IN KETOGENIC DIETS:

Foods to consume regularly:

- Seafood including salmon, sardines, crabs, shrimp and tuna. Fatty food is great!

- Meat, including lamb, pork, beef, chicken and turkey

- Dairy products, including milk, yogurt and cheese. Remember that flavoured yogurt may contain extra sugars.

- Eggs are high in protein and I w in s tur t d f t which means you r I ss lik I t feel hunger

- Fresh leafy vegetables including kale, spinach, broccoli, cauliflower, cucumber, turnips, lettuce, asparagus.

- Nuts and seeds are allowed but try to control your intake since they also have lots of calories. Avoid cashew nuts.

- Tea and coffee are both great but without sugar, you may want to opt for a natural sweetener alternative.

- Dark chocolate with at least 80% cocoa

Foods to avoid:

- Limit the intake of fruits because of their high levels of sugar

- White starches only add empty calories

- Avoid alcohol, it contains unnecessary and unhealthy sugars

CHAPTER 3 / CHAFFLES NUTRITION AND CARB COUNT

You can easily prepare two waffles with one large egg and half a cup of shredded cheese. Obviously, the carb and calorie intake will change slightly according to the type of cheese you're using. Generally speaking, chaffles will be entirely carb-free if you use whole milk cheese, such as mozzarella or cheddar, instead of American cheese or cream cheese which may contain a small amount of carbs. Usually, a 2-chaffles serving would contain 300 Calories, 0 carbohydrates, 20 grams of fats and 25 grams of protein. They are perfect as keto-friendly food. High in protein and fat and zero carbs. Cheese and eggs, and both are excellent sources of high-quality protein. Cheese also provides the body with plenty of calcium. Just two chaffles can provide 80% of the body's daily calcium requirements, which is great.

CHAPTER 4 / FEW TIPS FOR DELICIOUS WAFFLES

Here you can find few tips that will help you prepare delicious chaffle.

- Add a slice or two of ground ham while blending the cheese and the eggs. Ham will add more protein and flavor to your meal. If you are on a strict ketogenic regime, you may want to use bacon instead.
- Before you add the batter, sprinkle some cheese on your waffle iron to have a crispier result.
- Do not open the waffle maker too soon for checking. It should continue cooking until the chaffle is golden brown.
- Use almond/coconut flour! Coconut flour will give your chaffles a bread-like texture, especially if you're preparing a sweet chaffle. Almond flour, will reduce the eggy flavor and will give a better texture.
- Use mozzarella cheese if you prefer your chaffles sweet and opt for cheddar cheese for savory ones. You can also try using Haloumi or goat cheese for a more intense flavour. Keep in mind that goat cheese is generally more difficult to digest. Pepper Jack cheese will give a slightly tangy taste.

CHAPTER 5 — CHAFFLE MAKER CLEANING ROUTINE

Once the waffle iron cools down, wipe the surface with a damp cloth or paper towel to remove all that can be brushed off without too much hassle, crumbs usually. Pour a few drops of cooking oil on the batter to remove the stubborn batter drips. Allow it to sit for a few minutes. Next, grab some non-abrasive dish soap and hot water to rub the plates. You may want to use a toothbrush as well to clean in between the holes.
Never forget that your waffle maker is an electric machine, don't submerge it in water to clean it. Ensure that the waffle maker is completely dry before storing it.

CHAFFLE MAKER MAINTENANCE TIPS

Here are some tips to maintain your precious waffle maker, if you follow them correctly you won't have to replace it every now and then.
1- Before you use the machine for the first time, remember to cautiously read the manual. Every Waffle maker has its own rules, its own temperatures and its own cleaning routine.
2- Modern Waffle irons have nonsticky surfaces so that require only a light coat of cooking oil. If you can get a non-Stick cooking oil sprays it will be easier and quicker to coat the surface. Unlike pans, waffle irons does not present a smooth surface, it will be difficult to coat it with regular oil.
3- Never use a metal utensil to turn or remove your chaffles, they can damage the nonstick surface of the waffle iron. I recommend a silicon spatula or, in case you don't have one, a wooden utensil will work just fine.
4- Clean your waffle maker after every use as explained before.

EASY BASIC CHAFFLE

INGREDIENTS

- 1 cup mozzarella cheese, melted
- 1/2 cup egg whites

NUTRITION

Protein: 36% 42 kcal, Fat: 60% 71 kcal, Carbohydrates: 4%

HOW TO MAKE IT

1. Turn on your square waffle iron. Mist with nonstick spray.
2. Whip the egg whites with a mixer, until fluffy and white.
3. Pour in the cheese and mix well. Add the batter into the waffle iron.
4. Shut the machine and cook for about 3 minutes. Continue with the rest of the batter.
5. Take the waffles out of the machine.
6. Serve hot and enjoy!

 SERVINGS: 2

 COOKING TIME: 5 MINUTES

COCOBERRY CHAFFLE

INGREDIENTS

- 1 egg white
- 1/4 cup parmesan, shredded
- 1/4 cup jack cheese, shredded
- 1 tsp coconut flour
- 1/2 tsp stevia
- 1/4 tsp baking powder
- 2 tbsps. coconut flour
- 4 oz. raspberries
- 1 oz blackberry
- 2 oz. unsweetened raspberry sauce
- 1 tsp coconut, grated

HOW TO MAKE IT

1. Preheat your round waffle maker and once hot grease it with cooking spray.
2. Mix all chaffle ingredients in a bowl and combine with a whisk or fork. Pour chaffle batter into the maker and close the lid.
3. Once ready, place the chaffle on a board and roll the chaffle with a kitchen roller; set it aside and allow it to set for a few minutes. When the chaffle is set, remove it gently from the roller.
4. Dip raspberries in sauce and arrange on taco chaffle. Drizzle coconut flour and grated coconut on top.

 SERVINGS: 2

 COOKING TIME: 5 MINUTES

NUTRITION

77 kcal, Protein: 28% Fat: 6 187 kcal Carbohydrates: 3%

ALMOND BAGEL CHAFFLES

INGREDIENTS

- ½ cup mozzarella
- 2 eggs
- 1 tsp bagel seasoning
- ½ cup parmesan cheese
- 2 teaspoons almond flour

HOW TO MAKE IT

1. Put the chaffle maker to heat and grease it with cooking spray.
2. Spread half of the cheeses evenly on the griddle and let them melt. Next, toast for 30 seconds and let them wait for the batter.
3. Beat the eggs, the other half of the cheeses, the almond flour and the muffin seasoning in a small bowl.
4. Transfer the batter into the waffle iron.
5. Cook for a few minutes. Cool for 2-3 minutes before serving.

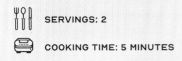

SERVINGS: 2

COOKING TIME: 5 MINUTES

NUTRITION

Carbs: 18g, Fat: 20 g, Protein: 21 g, Calories: 287.

VANILLA SOFT CHAFFLE

INGREDIENTS

- 1 egg white
- 1/4 cup parmesan, shredded
- 1/4 cup jack cheese, shredded
- 1 tsp coconut flour
- 1/2 tsp stevia
- 1/4 tsp baking powder
- 2 tbsps. coconut flour
- 4 oz. raspberries
- 1 oz blackberry
- 2 oz. unsweetened raspberry sauce
- 1 tsp coconut, grated

HOW TO MAKE IT

1. Preheat and grease a mini waffle iron.
2. Place the egg and vanilla extract in a bowl and whisk until well mixed.
3. Add the flour, baking, cinnamon, clove, powder and mix thoroughly. Add the half Mozzarella cheese and stir to combine.
4. In a small bowl, place the egg and the rest of Mozzarella cheese and stir to combine.
5. Place half of this mixture into the preheated waffle iron and cook for about 5-minutes or until brown and crispy.
6. Repeat the process with the remaining mixture to make another one.
7. Serve before it gets cold!

SERVINGS: 2

COOKING TIME: 5 MINUTES

NUTRITION

Calories: 103, Net Carb: 2.4g, Fat: 6.6g, ,Saturated Fat: 2.3g, Carbohydrates: 2g, Dietary Fiber: 0.5g, Sugar: 0.6g, Protein: 6.8g

BUTTERY CEREAL CHAFFLE

INGREDIENTS

- 1 egg
- 1/8 teaspoon sweetener
- 1 tablespoon sweetener
- ¼ teaspoon vanilla extract
- ½ teaspoon coconut flour
- 2 tablespoons almond flour
- ¼ teaspoon baking powder

HOW TO MAKE IT

1. Plug in your waffle maker and preheat it.
2. Put all the ingredients in a bowl.
3. Stir them together until well blended.
4. Let the batter rest for 2 minutes before cooking.
5. Dump half of the batter into the waffle iron.
6. Heat and cook for 4 minutes. Prepare the next chaffle following the same steps.

 SERVINGS: 4

 COOKING TIME: 7—9 MINUTES

NUTRITION

Nutrition Info per Servings: Calories 154, Total Fat 21.2g, Cholesterol

---

KETO PROTEIN CHAFFLE

INGREDIENTS

- ½ tsp vanilla extract
- ½ cup whey protein powder
- 3 tbsp sour cream
- 1 beaten egg
- A pinch of salt
- 1 tsp baking powder
- Topping:
- 1 tbsp natural sweetener
- 2 tbsp heavy cream

NUTRITION

Calories 164, Protein 41.6g, Carbs 13.1g 5%, Fat 25.9g 33%, Sugars 2.1g.

 SERVINGS: 4

 COOKING TIME: 7—9 MINUTES

HOW TO MAKE IT

1. Plug in the waffle iron to preheat it and coat it with non-stick cooking spray.
2. In one mixing bowl, mix together the egg, vanilla and sour cream. In another mixing bowl, combine the protein powder, baking powder and salt.
3. Add the flour mixture to the egg mixture and blend until the ingredients are well incorporated and you have a smooth batter.
4. Then pour an adequate amount of the batter into the waffle maker and place the batter to the edges to fill all the holes in the waffle iron.
5. Close the waffle maker and cook the waffles for about 4 minutes or depending on the settings of your waffle iron.
6. When cooked, use a plastic or silicone utensil to remove the waffles from the waffle iron.
7. Keep repeating steps 4 to 6 until you have baked all the batter into chaffles.
8. To make the topping, whisk the cream and icing sugar powder in a mixing bowl until smooth and fluffy.
9. Garnish the waffles with the cream and enjoy!

SWEET CHAFFLES BAKED IN THE OVEN

INGREDIENTS

- 2 cups mozzarella cheese
- 3 eggs
- 1 tsp stevia
- ¼ cup coconut flour
- 1 tbsp. coconut cream
- 1 tbsp. coconut oil
- 1 tsp. baking powder

HOW TO MAKE IT

1. The oven should be preheated to 4000F.
2. Combine the ingredients in a medium bowl. Transfer the batter to a silicone waffle mould and put on a baking tray.
3. Bake the waffles in the oven for approximately 10-15 minutes. When baked, remove from oven, serve hot with coffee and enjoy!

 SERVINGS: 2

 COOKING TIME: 5 MINUTES

NUTRITION

Nutrition Info per Servings: Carbohydrates: 5% 276 kcal, Protein: 34%

PEANUT CHOCOLATE CHAFFLE

INGREDIENTS

- Filling:
- 3 tbsp all-natural peanut butter
- 2 tsp stevia
- 1 tsp vanilla extract
- 2 tbsp heavy cream
- Chaffle:
- ¼ tsp baking powder

HOW TO MAKE IT

1. Chaffle: Plug the waffle maker, preheat it and spray it with a non-stick spray.
2. In a large mixing bowl, combine the almond flour, cocoa powder, baking powder and natural sweetener.
3. Add the egg, vanilla extract and heavy cream. Mix until the ingredients are well combined and you form a smooth batter.
4. Pour some of the batter into the preheated waffle maker. Spread out the batter to the borders of the waffle maker to cover the entire space on the waffle iron.
5. Close the lid and bake for about 5 minutes or according to waffle maker's settings.

 SERVINGS: 2

 COOKING TIME: 5 MINUTES

NUTRITION

277 kcal, Protein: 28% Fat: 6 187 kcal Carbohydrates: 3%

MORNING COFFEE CHAFFLE

INGREDIENTS

- ½ tsp. vanilla extract
- 6 tbsp. strong boiled espresso
- 4 ounces cream cheese
- Pinch of salt
- 4 eggs
- 1 tsp. baking powder
- ¼ cup stevia

HOW TO MAKE IT

1. Prepare the waffle iron. Place the eggs and cream cheese in a bowl and add the vanilla extract, espresso, almond flour, stevia, pinch of salt and baking powder.
2. Mix until everything is combined and fully incorporated.
3. Butter the heated waffle iron and add a few spoonfuls of the batter.
4. Depending on your waffle iron, cook for about 7-8 minutes.
5. Serve and enjoy!

SERVINGS: 4

COOKING TIME: 7—9 MINUTES

NUTRITION

Calories 300, Carbohydrates 4.8 g, Fat 26.g, Sodium 235 mg, Sugar 0.5

SCRAMBLED EGGS & ONIONS CHAFFLE

INGREDIENTS

- 4 eggs
- 2 cups mozzarella cheese, grated
- 2 spring onions, finely chopped
- Salt and pepper to taste
- ½ tsp dried garlic powder
- 2 tbsp almond flour
- 2 tbsp coconut flour
- For the scrambled eggs:
- 2 tbsp butter for brushing
- 6-8 eggs
- Salt and pepper
- 1 tsp Italian spice mix
- 1 tbsp olive oil
- 1 tbsp freshly chopped parsley

HOW TO MAKE IT

1. Preheat the waffle maker and in the meanwhile crack the eggs into a bowl and add the grated cheese. Whisk until well combined, then add the chopped spring onions.
2. Season with salt, pepper, and dried garlic powder.
3. Mix in the almond flour until everything is blended.
4. Brush the heated waffle maker with butter and add a few tablespoons of the batter.
5. Close the lid and cook for about 7–8 minutes.
6. While it is cooking, prepare the scrambled eggs by whisking the

SERVINGS: 4

COOKING TIME: 9 MINUTES

NUTRITION

Calories 194, fat 14.7 g, carbs 5 g, sugar 0.6 g, Protein 1 g, sodium 191 mg

KETOGENIC COCOA PROTEIN CHAFFLE

INGREDIENTS

- 3 tsp unsweetened Cocoa powder
- 1 egg (beaten)
- 3 tbsp sour cream
- 1 tsp baking powder
- A pinch of salt
- ½ cup whey protein powder
- Topping:
- 1 tbsp granulated natural sweetener
- 2 tbsp heavy cream

SERVINGS: 1

COOKING TIME: 8 MINUTES

HOW TO MAKE IT

1. Plug in the waffle iron to get it preheated and spray it with non-stick cooking spray.
2. Meanwhile, in a mixing bowl, mix together the egg, vanilla and sour cream. In a separate mixing bowl, combine the protein powder, baking powder and salt.
3. Add the flour mixture to the egg mixture and whisk until the ingredients are combined well and you have a smooth batter.
4. Then pour an adequate amount of the batter into the waffle iron and distribute the batter to the edges in order to cover all the holes in the waffle iron.
5. Shut the waffle iron and bake the chaffles for approximately 4 minutes or depending on the settings of your chaffle iron.
6. When cooked, use a plastic or silicone utensil to remove the waffles from the waffle iron.
7. Continue to repeat steps 4 to 6 until you have cooked all the batter into waffles. To make the topping, in a mixing bowl, whisk together the cream and icing sugar powder until smooth and fluffy.
8. Garnish the waffles with the cream and enjoy.

NUTRITION

Calories 194, Fat 25.9g 33%, Carbohydrate 13.1g 5%, Sugars 2.1g, Protein 41.6g

BACON AND EGGS CHAFFLE

INGREDIENTS

- 1 cup mozzarella cheese, shredded
- 4 tablespoons almond flour
- 2 large organic eggs, beaten
- 1 teaspoon organic baking powder
- 4 cooked bacon stripes
- 4 organic fried eggs

SERVINGS: 4

COOKING TIME: 20 MINUTES

HOW TO MAKE IT

1. Warm up a mini waffle iron and then grease it. Place all the ingredients in a medium bowl and mix with a fork until well mixed.
2. Pour half of the mixture into the preheated waffle iron and cook for approximately 3-5 minutes.
3. Do the same with the rest of the mixture.
4. Serve each waffle with the topping ingredients

NUTRITION

Calories 197, Net Carb: 2g, Total Fat 14.5 g, Saturated Fat 4.1 g, Cholesterol 2 mg, Sodium 224 g, Total Carbs 2.7 g, Fiber 0.8 g, Sugar 0.8 g, Protein 12.9 g.

17

AVOCADO GRAND CHAFFLE

INGREDIENTS

- 4 tbsps. avocado mash
- 1/2 cup Halloumi or Feta cheese, shredded
- 2 eggs
- 1/2 tsp lemon juice
- 1/8 tsp salt
- 1/8 tsp black pepper

HOW TO MAKE IT

1. Mix the avocado mash with lemon juice, salt, and black pepper in a bowl, until properly combined.
2. In a second small bowl whip eggs and pour them in the avocado mixture and mix thoroughly.
3. Sprinkle 1/8 of shredded cheese in a preheated waffle maker and then pour ½ of egg and avocado mixture, plus 1/8 of shredded cheese.
4. Secure the lid and cook chaffles for about 3 - 4 minutes. Repeat with the remaining mixture.
5. In the meantime fry the eggs in a pan for about 1-2 minutes. For serving, arrange fried egg on the chaffle with avocado slices and tomatoes. Scatter salt and pepper on top as desired.

 SERVINGS: 4

 COOKING TIME: 7—9 MINUTES

NUTRITION

Protein: 26%, 266 kcal Fat: 67%, Carbohydrates: 6%, Protein 10.8 g.

SIMPLE TASTY CHAFFLE

INGREDIENTS

- 4 eggs
- 1 cup grated mozzarella cheese
- 1 cup grated provolone cheese
- ½ cup almond flour
- 2 tbsp coconut flour
- 2½ tbsp baking powder
- Batter
- Salt and pepper to taste
- 2 tbsp butter to brush the waffle maker
- 1 tbsp olive oil
- 1 tbsp freshly chopped parsley

HOW TO MAKE IT

1. Preheat your chaffle maker.
2. Add the grated mozzarella and your tasty provolone cheese to a bowl and mix.
3. Add the coconut flour, the almond flour, the baking powder and add just a pinch of salt and pepper. Whisk and carefully crack in the eggs.
4. Mix everything together until well amalgamated.
5. Brush the heated waffle maker with butter and add a few tablespoons of the batter.
6. Close the lid and cook for about 8 minutes depending on your waffle maker.
7. Serve and savor.

 SERVINGS: 4

 COOKING TIME: 7—9 MINUTES

NUTRITION

Calories 352, Fat 27.2 g, Carbs 8.3 g, Sugar 0.5 g, Protein 15 g, Sodium 442 mg

BACON CHAFFLE

INGREDIENTS

- 4 eggs
- 2 ounces finely chopped bacon
- 2 cups shredded mozzarella
- Salt and pepper to taste
- Batter
- 1 tsp dried oregano
- 2 tbsp olive oil for brushing the

HOW TO MAKE IT

1. Preheat the maker. Crack the eggs into a container and add the grated mozzarella cheese.
2. Mix until it's blended and sprinkle on it the chopped bacon.
3. Mix, add salt, pepper and dried oregano, just enough. Brush the heated waffle maker with olive oil and add a 2/3 tablespoons of the batter.
4. Close and cook for about 7–8 minutes. Enjoy!

 SERVINGS: 2

 COOKING TIME: 5 MINUTES

NUTRITION

Calories 241, Fat 19.8 g, Carbs 1.3 g, Sugar 0.4 g, Protein 14.8 g, Sodium 4 mg

BREAKFAST GREEN CHAFFLE

INGREDIENTS

- 1 egg
- 1 pinch of Italian seasoning
- 1/2 cup cheddar cheese, shredded
- 1 tbsp. pizza sauce
- Topping:
- 2 eggs boiled

HOW TO MAKE IT

1. Preheat your waffle maker and grease it with cooking spray. Crack an egg in a small bowl and whip it with Italian seasoning and pizza sauce.
2. Add shredded cheese to the mixture. Pour 1 tbsp. of shredded cheese in a waffle maker and cook for 30 sec. Pour the chaffles batter in the waffle maker and close the lid.
3. Cook chaffles for about 4 minute until crispy and brown.
4. Carefully remove chaffles from the maker.
5. Prepare a bed of spinach with boil egg, avocado slice, and tomatoes and place the chaffle on it, before serving. Enjoy!

 SERVINGS: 2

 COOKING TIME: 5 MINUTES

NUTRITION

Protein: 23% 277 kcal, Fat: 66% 222 kcal, Carbohydrates: 11%

FRESH BERRIES CHOCO CHAFFLES

INGREDIENTS

- 1 cup egg whites
- 1 cup cheddar cheese, shredded
- ¼ cup heavy cream
- ¼ cup almond flour

Topping:

- 4 oz. fresh raspberries
- 4 oz. fresh strawberries
- 1 oz. keto chocolate flakes
- 1 oz. feta cheese

NUTRITION

Protein: 28% 268 kcal Fat: 67% 163 kcal
Carbohydrates: 5%

 SERVINGS: 4

 COOKING TIME: 5 MINUTES

HOW TO MAKE IT

1. Preheat your square waffle maker and grease with cooking spray. Whisk egg whites in a small bowl with flour.
2. Add shredded cheese to the mixture until well mixed, then add cream and cheese, and stir gently.
3. Pour Chaffles batter in a waffle maker, close the lid and cook chaffles for about 4 minutes, until crispy and brown.
4. Carefully remove chaffles from the maker. Serve with berries, cheese, and chocolate flakes on top.
5. Enjoy!

BLT SANDWICH CHAFFLE

INGREDIENTS

- 1 egg
- 1/2 cup Cheddar cheese, shredded
- 2 strips bacon
- 1-2 slices tomato
- 3 pieces lettuce
- 1 tbsp mayonnaise
- Chaffle Ingredients:
- 2 whole eggs
- 4 oz. cheese
- 2 oz. almond flour
- 1/4 cup almond flour
- 1 tsp baking powder

  SERVINGS: 4

COOKING TIME: 10 MINUTES

HOW TO MAKE IT

1. Preheat the waffle maker. Mix together all the chaffle ingredients in a bowl.
2. Mix together egg and shredded cheese in a small mixing bowl and stir until well combined. Pour one half of the waffle batter into the waffle maker and cook for 4 minutes or until golden brown.
3. Repeat the process to make the second half of the sandwich.
4. Cook the bacon until crispy in a large pan over medium heat, turning as needed.
5. Remove and drain the bacon on paper towels.
6. Assemble the sandwich with lettuce, tomato, and mayonnaise and enjoy your lunch!

NUTRITION

Protein: 17g, Fat: 18g, Carbohydrates: 2g 12, Fiber 0g, 268 kcal

. . . .

LOBSTER BASIL CHAFFLE

INGREDIENTS

- ¼ tsp garlic powder
- 1 egg (beaten)
- 1/8 tsp Italian seasoning
- ¼ tsp onion powder
- ½ cup shredded mozzarella cheese

Lobster Filling:

- 1 tbsp chopped green onion
- ½ cup lobster tails (defrosted)
- 1 tsp dried basil
- 1 tbsp mayonnaise
- 1 tsp lemon juice

  SERVINGS: 2

COOKING TIME: 8 MINUTES

HOW TO MAKE IT

1. Connect the waffle iron to preheat it and spray it with non-stick cooking spray. Blend the mozzarella, Italian seasoning, garlic and onion powder in a mixing bowl. Include the egg and mix until well combined.
2. Add an appropriate quantity of batter to the waffle iron and spread the batter so that all the holes in the waffle iron are covered. Shut the waffle iron and bake the waffles for approx. 7 minutes or depending on the settings of your waffle iron. Once cooked, use a plastic or silicone utensil to remove the waffles and place them on a cooling rack.
3. Continue repeating steps 3 to 5 until you have baked all the batter into waffles.
4. To make the filling, place the lobster tail in a medium mixing bowl and add the mayonnaise, basil and lemon juice. Stir the ingredients until they are well mixed. Stuff the chaffles with the lobster mixture and garnish with chopped green onions. Serve and enjoy!

NUTRITION

Fat 6.3g 8%, Carbohydrate 3g 1%, Sugars 1g, Protein 11.9g, 248 kcal **2 1**

SALMON AND CREAM ALMOND CHAFFLES

INGREDIENTS

- 4 tbsp. heavy cream
- 4 oz. smoked salmon
- 1/2 medium onion sliced
- 2 tbsps. parsley chopped

CHAFFLE Ingredients:

- 2 tbsps. almond flour
- 1 tsp stevia
- 1 tsp vanilla
- 1/2 cup mozzarella cheese
- 1 egg

 SERVINGS: 4

 COOKING TIME: 20 MINUTES

HOW TO MAKE IT

1. Prepare 4 heart-shaped chaffles with the chaffle ingredients.
2. Place smoked salmon and heavy cream on every chaffle.
3. Garnish with onion slice and parsley.
4. Serve and enjoy!

NUTRITION

Protein: 34% 79 kcal, Fat: 60% 237 kcal, Carbohydrates: 6% 14 kcal.

- -

GARLIC CHAFFLES WITH HAM

INGREDIENTS

- 1/8 tsp Italian seasoning
- 1 scallion (chopped)
- ½ jalapeno pepper (chopped)
- 1 large egg
- ½ cup shredded mozzarella cheese
- ¼ tsp garlic salt
- 4 tbsp chopped ham steak

 SERVINGS: 1

 COOKING TIME: 5 MINUTES

HOW TO MAKE IT

1. Connect the waffle iron to preheat and spray with non-stick spray.
2. Combine the cheese, Italian seasoning, jalapeno, spring onions, ham and garlic salt in a mixing bowl. Include the egg and mix until well combined.
3. Stuff the waffle iron with an appropriate amount of the batter. Distribute the batter to the top of the waffle iron so that all the holes in the waffle iron are covered.
4. Shut the waffle iron and bake the waffles for approx. minutes or depending on the settings of the waffle iron.
5. Remove the waffles from the waffle iron with a plastic or silicone tool when cooked.
6. Serve and enjoy.

NUTRITION

Fat 10.6g 14%, Carbohydrate 4.3g 2%, Sugars 1.2g, Protein 16.4g. 269 kcal

NO CHAFFLE IRON CHAFFLES

INGREDIENTS

- 1 tbsp. avocado oil
- 1/2 cup cheddar cheese
- 1 tbsp. chia seeds
- A pinch of salt
- 1 egg waffle maker

Topping:
- 1 tbsp granulated natural sweetener
- 2 tbsp heavy cream

 SERVINGS: 2

 COOKING TIME: 5 MINUTES

HOW TO MAKE IT

1. Preheat your non-stick pan over medium heat. Combine chia seeds, salt, egg and cheese in a small bowl.
2. As soon as the pan is hot, add 2 tablespoons of chia batter and fry for about 1-2 minutes. Flip and fry for another 1-2 minutes.
3. As soon as the waffles are brown, remove from the pan.
4. Serve with berries sprinkled on top and enjoy.

NUTRITION

Protein: 19% 244 kcal, Fat: % 181 kcal, Carbohydrates: 1%

VEGGY AND TUNA CHAFFLES

INGREDIENTS

Tuna Sandwich:
- 1 small carrot (chopped)
- 1 celery stalk (chopped)
- 1 small sweet onion (chopped)
- ¼ tsp salt or to taste
- 1 green bell pepper (chopped)
- 1 can water packed tuna
- ¼ tsp ground black pepper
- 1 tbsp freshly chopped parsley
- 2 tbsp mayonnaise
- ½ tsp paprika

Chaffle:
- ½ tsp garlic powder
- 1 cup shredded mozzarella
- ¾ tsp baking powder
- 2 eggs (beaten)
- 4 tbsp almond flour

 SERVINGS: 2

 COOKING TIME: 8 MINUTES

HOW TO MAKE IT

1. Connect the waffle iron to preheat it and spray it with non-stick cooking spray.
2. Blend the almond flour, baking powder, garlic powder and mozzarella in a mixing bowl. Include the eggs and blend the ingredients until well combined.
3. Put an appropriate amount of the batter into the waffle iron and distribute the batter to the edges to cover all the holes in the waffle iron. Shut the waffle iron and cook the waffles for approx. 7 minutes or depending on the settings of the waffle iron.
4. When done cooking, use a silicone or plastic utensil to take the waffles out of the waffle iron. Continue repeating steps 3 to 5 until you have baked all the batter into waffles.
5. Combine tuna, celery, pepper, onion, salt, paprika, carrot and green pepper in a mixing bowl.
6. Include the mayonnaise and toss until well mixed. Set one of the chaffs on a flat surface and spoon ½ of the tuna salad into it.
7. Place some fresh parsley on top. Top with another chaff and press down firmly.
8. To make the second sandwich, repeat the step.
9. Serve and enjoy.

NUTRITION

Fat 26.3g 34%, Carbohydrate 19.6g 7%, Sugars 7.7g, Protein 37.8g, 298 kcal

DOUBLE CHEESE TACO CHAFFLE

INGREDIENTS

- 1 egg white
- tsp chili powder
- Pinch of salt
- 1 tsp coconut flour
- ¼ cup shredded Monterey jack cheese
- ¼ cup shredded sharp cheddar cheese
- ¼ tsp baking powder

HOW TO MAKE IT

1. Heat the waffle iron and spray it with cooking spray. Blend all the components in a bowl.
2. Dump half of the batter into the waffle iron and cook for 4 minutes. Take out the waffles and set aside.
3. Do the same with the rest of the waffle batter. Flip a muffin tin over and place the chaffle between the cups to form a shell. Allow to set for 2-4 minutes.
4. Transfer to a muffin tin and serve with your favorite taco recipe.

 SERVINGS: 1

 COOKING TIME: 8 MINUTES

NUTRITION

Carbs: 4 g, Fat: 19 g, Protein: 18 g, Calories: 258

ITALIAN STYLE PEPPERONI CHAFFLES

INGREDIENTS

- ¼ teaspoon garlic powder
- 6 turkey pepperoni slices, chopped
- ¼ teaspoon onion powder
- ½ teaspoon Italian seasoning
- ¼ cup Mozzarella cheese, shredded
- 2 tablespoons Parmesan cheese, grated
- ¼ cup cauliflower rice
- 1 organic egg, beaten
- ¼ cup Cheddar cheese, shredded

HOW TO MAKE IT

1. Preheat a mini waffle iron and pregrease it.
2. Put all ingredients in a medium bowl and mix until well combined.
3. Drop ¼ of the mixture into the preheated waffle iron and cook for about 4 minutes or until golden brown.
4. Continue with the rest of the mixture.
5. Serve hot and enjoy!

 SERVINGS: 4

 COOKING TIME: 16 MINUTES

NUTRITION

Calories: 203, Net Carb: 0.4g, Fat: 8g, Saturated Fat: 3.2g,
Carbohydrates: 0.8g, Dietary Fiber: 0.2g, Sugar: 0.4g, Protein: 10.2g

JALAPENO PEPPER TORTILLA CHAFFLE

INGREDIENTS

- ½ cup cheddar cheese, shredded
- 1 tsp. baking powder
- Sour cream
- 1 egg
- Jalapeno pepper, chopped
- 1 tbsp. almond milk
- 4 tbsp. almond flour
- ¼ tsp. garlic powder
- Homemade salsa waffle maker

HOW TO MAKE IT

1. Preheat your waffle iron. In a bowl, beat the egg. Mix in the cheese, baking powder, flour, garlic powder and almond milk.
2. Pour half of the batter into the waffle iron.
3. Close the lid and cook for 4 minutes. Open and transfer to a plate. Allow to cool for 2 minutes.
4. Repeat with the rest of the batter.
5. Cover the waffle with the sauce, sour cream and jalapeño bell pepper.
6. Wrap the waffle.

SERVINGS: 2

COOKING TIME: 8 MINUTES

NUTRITION

Calories 225 Dietary Fiber 0.8g Saturated Fat 9.9g Cholesterol 117mg

---

LETTUCE AND YOGURT SAUCE CHAFFLE

INGREDIENTS

- 4 lettuce leaves
- 1 tbsp. almond flour
- 1/8 tsp baking powder
- 1 large egg
- 1 tbsp. full-fat Greek yogurt
- 1/4 cup shredded Swiss cheese

HOW TO MAKE IT

1. Turn on your waffle iron. Lubricate it with cooking spray.
2. Combine the egg, almond flour, yogurt, baking powder and cheese in a bowl.
3. Put 1/2 cup of the batter in the centre of your chaffle iron and shut the lid.
4. Roast the chaffles for about 2-3 minutes, until they are cooked through. Do the same with the rest of the batter.
5. When they are done, carefully transfer them to a plate.
6. Arrange lettuce leaves between 2 chaffles.
7. Serve and enjoy!

SERVINGS: 2

COOKING TIME: 5 MINUTES

NUTRITION

Carbohydrates: 12% 222 kcal, Fat: 66% 120 kcal, Protein: 22%

CHICKEN FEISTY CHAFFLE

INGREDIENTS

- 1 chicken breast, cut into 2 pieces
- 1/4 cup finely grated Parmesan
- 1/2 cup coconut flour
- 1/2 tsp. onion powder
- 1/2 tsp. garlic powder
- 1 tsp. paprika
- 1 tsp. salt & pepper
- 1 egg beaten
- Avocado oil for frying
- Lettuce leaves
- BBQ sauce
- Chaffle Ingredients:
- 2 whole eggs
- 4 oz. cheese
- 2 oz. almond flour

HOW TO MAKE IT

1. Mix together all the chaffle ingredients in a bowl.
2. Pour the chaffle batter in a preheated greased square maker.
3. Cook the chaffles for about 2-minutes until lightly browned.
4. Meanwhile mix together coconut flour, parmesan, paprika, onion powder, garlic powder, salt and pepper in a bowl. Dip chicken in this mixture first then in the beaten egg.
5. Heat avocado oil in a skillet and cook the chicken both sides until lightly brown.
6. Arrange the chicken between two chaffles, with lettuce and BBQ sauce... and treat yourself!

NUTRITION

Protein: 30% 219 kcal, Fat: 60% 435 kcal, Carbohydrates: 9% 66 kcal

 SERVINGS: 2

 COOKING TIME: 15 MINUTES

CHEESE & BACON CHAFFLE

INGREDIENTS

- 1 egg
- 1/2 cup cheddar cheese
- 1 tbsp. parmesan cheese
- 3/4 tsp coconut flour
- 1/4 tsp baking powder
- 1/8 tsp Italian Seasoning
- pinch of salt
- 1/4 tsp garlic powder
- For Topping:
- 1 bacon sliced, cooked and chopped
- 1/2 cup provolone cheese
- 1/4 tsp parsley, chopped

HOW TO MAKE IT

1. Preheat oven to 400 degrees.
2. Mix together chaffle ingredients in a mixing bowl until well combined. Spoon half of the batter in the center of the waffle maker (greased with cooking spray) and close the lid.
3. Cook the chaffles for about 3 minutes until cooked.
4. Carefully remove the chaffles from the maker and arrange them in a greased baking tray.
5. Top with provolone cheese, chopped bacon, parsley and bake in the oven for 5 minutes or once the cheese is melted.
6. Remove carefully from the oven and enjoy!

 SERVINGS:2

 COOKING TIME: 15 MINUTES

NUTRITION

Protein: 28% 290 kcal Fat: 69% 222 kcal Carbohydrates: 3% kcal

EGG AND PEPPER CHAFFLES

INGREDIENTS

- For the egg:
- 1 small red bell pepper
- 4 large eggs
- 1 small green bell pepper
- 1 tbsp olive oil
- Salt to taste
- 2 tbsp grated Parmesan cheese
- ground black pepper to taste
- For the chaffles:
- 2 eggs, beaten
- 1 cup finely grated cheddar cheese

 SERVINGS: 4

 COOKING TIME: 28 MINUTES

HOW TO MAKE IT

1. For the waffles: Preheat the waffle iron.
2. Combine the egg with the cheddar in a medium bowl.
3. Pour in a quarter of the mixture in the maker, and cook until crisp, 6 to 7 minutes.
4. Make three more chaffles with the remaining mixture.
5. For the egg : In the meantime, heat the olive oil in a skillet over medium heat on the stovetop.
6. Whisk the eggs in a medium bowl with the peppers, salt, black pepper and Parmesan cheese.
7. Transfer the mixture to the skillet and stir for 2 minutes or until it is to your liking. In between two chaffles, spoon in half of the scrambled eggs and repeat with the second set of chaffles.

NUTRITION

Calories 387, Carbs 18, Net Carbs 17.52g, Fats 22.52g, Protein 27.76g

AVOCADO CHAFFLE

INGREDIENTS

- ½ avocado, sliced
- ½ tsp lemon juice
- tsp salt
- tsp black pepper
- 1 egg ½ cup shredded cheese
- ¼ crumbled feta cheese
- 1 cherry tomato, halved

 SERVINGS: 2

 COOKING TIME: 10 MINUTES

HOW TO MAKE IT

1. Mash together avocado, salt, pepper and lemon juice, until well-mixed.
2. Turn on your waffle maker to heat and spread with cooking spray.
3. Beat egg in a small mixing bowl. Place cup of cheese on waffle maker, then spread half of the egg mixture over it and top with cup of cheese.
4. Close and cook for 3-4 minutes. Repeat for remaining batter.
5. Let chaffles cool for 3-4 minutes, then spread avocado mix on top of each.
6. Top with crumbled feta and cherry tomato halves.

NUTRITION

Carbs: 5 g ;Fat: 19 g ;Protein: 7 g ;Calories: 232

MEXICAN CHAFFLE NACHOS

INGREDIENTS

- 1 cup finely grated Mexican cheese blend
- 2 eggs, beaten
- For the chicken-cheese topping:
- 2 cups cooked and diced chicken breasts
- 2 tbsp butter
- 2 tbsp hot sauce
- 1 cup finely grated cheddar cheese more to garnish
- 1 tbsp almond flour
- 2 tbsp chopped fresh scallions
- ¼ cup almond milk
- 3 bacon slices, cooked and chopped

 SERVINGS: 4

 COOKING TIME: 33 MINUTES

HOW TO MAKE IT

1. For the chaffles: Preheat the waffle iron. Combine the eggs and Mexican cheese mixture in a medium bowl.
2. Open the iron and add one-fourth of the mixture. Close and cook until crisp, approximately 7 minutes. Transfer the chaffle to a plate and make 3 more chaffles in the same way.
3. Arrange the chaffles on serving plates and set aside to serve.
4. For the chicken and cheese topping: melt the butter in a large skillet and stir in the almond flour until golden brown, about 1 minute.
5. Add the almond milk and whisk until well combined.
6. Simmer until thickened, 2 minutes. Stir in cheese to melt, 2 minutes, then stir in bacon, chicken and hot sauce.
7. Place the mixture over the chamfers and top with a little more cheddar cheese.
8. Decorate with the scallions and serve immediately.

NUTRITION

Calories 524, Fats 37.51g, Carbs 3.55g, Net Carbs 3.25g, Protein 41.86g.

....

AVOCADO SHRIMP CHAFFLE

INGREDIENTS

- ½ tsp curry powder
- 2 cups mozzarella cheese
- 4 large eggs
- ½ tsp oregano
- Shrimp Sandwich Filling:
- 1-pound raw shrimp
- 1 large avocado (diced)
- ½ tsp paprika
- 1 red bell pepper (diced)
- 2 tbsp sour cream
- ¼ cup onion (finely chopped)
- 1 tsp Cajun seasoning
- 1 tbsp olive oil
- 4 slices cooked bacon

HOW TO MAKE IT

1. Plug in the waffle iron to preheat it and spray it with nonstick spray.
2. Crack the eggs into a bowl and whisk them. Add the cheese, oregano and curry.
3. Mix until the ingredients are well combined. Pour an adequate amount of the batter into the chaffle maker and place the batter to the edges to cover all the holes in the waffle iron. This should make 8 mini waffles.
4. Close the chaffle maker and cook for a few minutes or according to your chaffle maker settings.
5. When the cooking cycle is complete, use a silicone or plastic utensil to remove the waffles from the chaffle iron. Repeat steps 3 through 5 until you have cooked all the batter in the chaffle.
6. Heat the olive oil over medium to high heat. Place the shrimp in the pan and cook until pink and tender.
7. Remove the skillet from the heat and use a skimmer to transfer the shrimp to a paper towel-lined plate to drain for a few minutes. Transfer the shrimp to a mixing bowl.

8. Add the paprika and Cajun seasoning. Toss until the shrimp are coated with the seasoning.
9. In order to assemble the sandwich, place a chamfer on a flat surface and spread some sour cream on it.
10. Arrange the shrimp, onion, avocado, diced bell bell pepper and a slice of bacon on top. Cover with another layer.
11. Continue with step 10 until you have assembled all the ingredients into sandwiches.
12. Serve and enjoy!

HOT DOG MUSTARD CHAFFLES

INGREDIENTS

- Mustard dressing for topping
- 8 pickle slices
- 1 cup finely grated cheddar cheese
- 1 egg, beaten
- 2 hot dog sausages, cooked

HOW TO MAKE IT

1. Prepare the waffle iron.
2. Combine the egg and cheddar cheese in a medium bowl.
3. Then open the iron and pour in half of the mixture. Shut it and cook for 7 minutes until a crispy waffle is formed.
4. Remove the waffle to a plate and make a second waffle in the same way.
5. In order to serve, cover each waffle with a sausage, put the mustard dressing on top and then add the cucumber slices on top.
6. Enjoy!

SERVINGS: 2

COOKING TIME: 14 MINUTES

NUTRITION

Calories 231, Fats 18.29g, Carbs 2.8g, Net Carbs 2.6g, Protein 13.39g.

MONTEREY CHEDDAR SLICES CHAFFLES

INGREDIENTS

- 1 large organic egg, beaten
- 2 ounces monterey cheddar cheese, cut into thin triangle slices

HOW TO MAKE IT

1. Warm a waffle iron beforehand and then butter it.
2. Arrange 1 thin layer of cheese slices on the base of the preheated waffle iron. Put the beaten egg on top of the cheese.
3. Place another layer of cheese slices on top now to evenly cover. Cook for approximately 6 minutes or until they are golden brown.
4. Serve warm and enjoy!

NUTRITION

Calories: 292, Net Carb: 2.4g, Fat: 23g, Saturated Fat: 13.6g, Carbohydrates: 2.4g, Dietary Fiber: 0g, Sugar: 0.4g, Protein: 18.3g. 113.3mg, Sodium 96.9mg, Potassium 453 mg, Saturated Fat 10g, Total Carbohydrate 5.9g.

  SERVINGS: 3

COOKING TIME: 6 MINUTES

BBQ SAUCE CHAFFLE

INGREDIENTS

- ¼ teaspoon baking powder
- 1 egg, beaten
- ½ teaspoon barbecue sauce
- ½ cup cheddar cheese, shredded

HOW TO MAKE IT

1. Connect your waffle iron to preheat it. Combine all the ingredients in a bowl. Add half of the ingredients to your waffle iron.
2. Put a lid on it and let it bake for a few minutes.
3. Do the same steps for the next grilled waffle.

  SERVINGS: 4

COOKING TIME: 9 MINUTES

NUTRITION

Calories 295, Total Fat 23 g, Saturated Fat 13 g, Cholesterol 223 mg, Sodium 414 mg, Potassium 179 mg, Total Carbohydrate 2 g, Dietary Fiber 1 g, Protein 20 g, Total Sugars 1 g.

GARLIC AND BASIL CHAFFLES

INGREDIENTS

- 1/4 tsp garlic powder
- 1 tbsp softened butter
- 1/2 cup Mozzarella cheese, shredded
- 1/2 tsp basil leaves
- 1 tbsp almond flour
- 1/4 cup shredded mozzarella cheese
- 1 egg
- 1/4 tsp garlic powder

SERVINGS: 4

COOKING TIME: 11 MINUTES

HOW TO MAKE IT

1. Heat the Waffle Iron. Combine your egg, basil, garlic, mozzarella cheese, almond flour and in a small bowl.
2. Add half of the batter to your mini waffle iron and bake for 4 minutes. When the waffles are not fully cooked, let them cook for another 2 minutes.
3. Next, cook the rest of the batter to create a second chaffle. Into a small bowl, combine 1 tablespoon of butter and garlic powder and place in the microwave to melt. This takes about 25 seconds, according to your microwave oven.
4. Place the chaffles on a tray and spread the butter-garlic mixture over the top with a brush made of rubber.
5. Sprinkle the cheese on top of each Chaffle.
6. Transfer the Chaffles to the oven at 400 degrees.
7. Bake until the cheese melts down.

NUTRITION

231kcal, Carbohydrates:2g, Sugar: 1g, Protein: 13g, Fat: 19g, Sodium: 346mg, Saturated Fat:10g, Cholesterol:130mg

LOW CARB CHAFFLE

INGREDIENTS

- 1/2 cup cheddar cheese, shredded
- 1 egg

SERVINGS: 2

COOKING TIME: 5 MINUTES

HOW TO MAKE IT

1. Turn on or plug in the waffle iron to heat and grease both sides.
2. Beat an egg in a small bowl, then pour in 1 cup of cheddar cheese and mix the batter. Then pour half of the batter into the waffle iron and close the lid.
3. Bake the chaffles for 3 minutes or until they are cooked to the desired crispness.
4. Carefully remove from the waffle iron and put aside for 2-3 minutes to make them crispy.
5. Repeat the procedure to prepare the second waffle.
6. Serve and enjoy!

NUTRITION

Calories: 291kcal, Carbohydrates:1g, Sodium:413mg, Protein: 20g, Sugar: 1g, Fat: 23g, Saturated Fat:13g, Cholesterol:223mg, Potassium: 116mg, Vitamin A: 804IU, Calcium: 432mg, Iron: 1mg.

CHEESY CAULIFLOWER CHAFFLE

INGREDIENTS

- ¼ tsp nutmeg
- ¼ tsp Italian seasoning
- ¼ tsp garlic powder
- 1 tbsp melted butter
- 1/8 tsp ground black pepper
- 1 cup cauliflower rice
- 1/8 tsp white pepper or to taste
- ½ cup shredded mozzarella cheese
- 1 egg
- ½ cup shredded parmesan cheese
- ¼ tsp salt or to taste
- ¼ tsp cinnamon
- Garnish:
- Chopped green onions

SERVINGS: 2

COOKING TIME: 8 MINUTES

HOW TO MAKE IT

1. Add ¼ of the Parmesan cheese to a blender, along with the mozzarella cheese, butter, egg, added salt, nutmeg, cinnamon, garlic powder, black pepper, white pepper, Italian seasoning and cauliflower.
2. Include the egg and mix until a smooth batter is formed. Connect the chaffle iron and preheat it.
3. Coat the waffle iron with a non-stick spray. Spread about a tablespoon of the remaining Parmesan on the chaffle.
4. Fill the waffle iron with ¼ of the batter and distribute the batter so that all the holes in the waffle iron are covered.
5. Spread some grated Parmesan over the batter. Shut the lid of the waffle iron and bake the waffles for about 4 to 5 minutes or depending on the settings of your waffle iron.
6. When finished cooking, take off the waffle with a rubber or silicone utensil.
7. Continue repeating steps until you have cooked all the batter into waffles. Serve and enjoy!

NUTRITION

Fat 15.8g 20%, Carbohydrate 6.2g 2%, Sugars 2.4g. Protein 15g, 278 kcal

GRUYERE CHEESE AND BACON CHAFFLES WITH

INGREDIENTS

Chaffles
- 1 tablespoon jalapeño pepper, chopped
- ½ cup Gruyere cheese, shredded
- 2 tablespoons cooked bacon pieces
- 1 organic egg, beaten

Dip
- Pinch of ground black pepper
- ¼ cup heavy cream
- ¼ teaspoon fresh dill, minced

SERVINGS: 2

COOKING TIME: 10 MINUTES

HOW TO MAKE IT

1. Warm up a mini waffle iron and then butter it. For the waffles: Place all the ingredients in a medium bowl and blend well.
2. Put half of the mixture into the preheated waffle iron and cook for about 5 minutes. Do the same with the rest of the mixture.
3. In the meantime, for the dip: Combine the cream and stevia in a bowl. Then serve the warm chaffles together with the dip.

NUTRITION

Calories 210, Net Carbs 2.2 g, Total Fat 13 g, Saturated Fat 9.7 g, Cholesterol 132 mg, Sodium 164 mg, Total Carbs 2.3 g, Fiber 0.1 g, Sugar 0.7 g, Protein 11.9 g.

SANDWICH CHAFFLE

INGREDIENTS

Chaffles
- 1 large organic egg, beaten
- ½ cup mozzarella cheese, shredded finely

Filling
- 4 tsp heavy cream
- 2 fresh strawberries, hulled and sliced
- 1 tsp fresh lemon juice
- 2 tbsp powdered erythritol
- Pinch of fresh lemon zest, grated

  SERVINGS: 2

COOKING TIME: 6 MINUTES

HOW TO MAKE IT

1. Preheat your waffle maker and grease it.
2. In a bowl, place all ingredients and whisk until everything is well combined. Place half of the mixture into preheated waffle maker and cook it for about 5–6 minutes.
3. Repeat the above process with the remaining mixture. Meanwhile, for filling: in a medium bowl, place the heavy cream, fresh lemon juice, powdered erythritol, whisk until the filling results well combined.
4. Serve each chaffle with cream mixture, strawberry slices and a sprinkle of lemon zest.

NUTRITION

Calories 295, Net Carbs 1.4 g Total Fat 5 g Saturated Fat 3.9 g Cholesterol 110 mg Sodium 82 mg Total Carbs 1.7 g Fiber 0.3 g Sugar 0.9 g Protein 5.5 g

TOMATO HAM SANDWICH CHAFFLES

INGREDIENTS

- 1 egg
- ½ cup cheese, shredded
- 1 tsp coconut flour
- Pinch of garlic powder

Filling
- 2 sugar-free ham slices
- 1 small tomato, sliced 2 lettuce

  SERVINGS: 2

COOKING TIME: 8 MINUTES

HOW TO MAKE IT

1. Preheat your waffle maker and make sure it is well greased.
2. In a bowl, place all ingredients and whisk until everything is well combined. Place half of the mixture into preheated waffle maker and cook it for about 5–6 minutes.
3. Repeat with the rest of the mixture. Serve each chaffle with filling ingredients.

NUTRITION

268 kcal Net Carbs 3.7 g Total Fat 8.7 g Saturated Fat 3.4 g Cholesterol 114 mg Sodium 794 mg Total Carbs 5.5 g Fiber 1.8 g Sugar 1.5 g
Protein 13.9 g

CHICKEN AND TOMATO CHAFFLES

INGREDIENTS

Chaffles

- 1 large egg, beaten
- ½ cup cheddar cheese, shredded
- Ground black pepper
- Pinch of salt

Filling

- 1 (around 6-ounce) pre-cooked chicken breast
- ¼ of small onion, sliced
- 2 lettuce leaves
- 1 tomato, sliced

  SERVINGS: 2

COOKING TIME: 8 MINUTES

HOW TO MAKE IT

1. Preheat your waffle maker and make sure it is well greased.
2. In a bowl, place all ingredients and whisk until everything is well combined. Place half of the mixture into preheated waffle maker and cook it for about 5–6 minutes.
3. Repeat with the rest of the mixture.
4. Once the chafes are ready, layer one half of your chicken breast, one lettuces leaf, onion to your likings and few tomato slices. Repeat the process with the remaining filling ingredients. Enjoy!

NUTRITION

248 kcal Net Carbs 2.5 g Total Fat 14.1 g Saturated Fat 6.8 g Cholesterol 177 mg Sodium 334 mg Total Carbs 3.3 g Fiber 0.8 g Sugar 2 g Protein 28.7 g

---

SAGE CHAFFLES

INGREDIENTS

- 1 organic egg
- ¾ cup coconut flour, sifted
- ½ cup cheddar cheese, shredded
- ¼ cup water
- 1 cup unsweetened coconut milk
- 1½ teaspoons organic baking powder
- ½ teaspoon dried ground sage
- 1/8 teaspoon garlic powder
- 1½ tablespoons coconut oil, melted
- 1/8 teaspoon salt

  SERVINGS: 6

COOKING TIME: 24 MINUTES

HOW TO MAKE IT

1. Preheat a waffle iron and grease it. Put the flour, baking powder, sage, garlic powder and salt in a bowl and mix well.
2. Mix in the egg, coconut milk, water and coconut oil until a stiff mixture is formed.
3. Add the cheese and mix softly to combine. Separate the mixture into 6 portions. Put a portion of the mixture in the preheated waffle iron and cook for about 4 minutes or until golden brown.
4. Continue with the rest of the batter.
5. Serve hot and enjoy!

NUTRITION

Calories: 247, Net Carb: 2.2g, Protein: 4g, Fat: 13g, Dietary Fiber: 0.7g, Saturated Fat: 10.7g, Carbohydrates: 2g,, Sugar: 1.3g.

DOUBLE CHEESE CHAFFLES

INGREDIENTS

- 1 organic egg
- ½ cup mozzarella cheese, shredded
- ¾ teaspoon coconut flour
- ¼ teaspoon organic baking powder
- 1 tablespoon Parmesan cheese, shredded
- Pinch of salt
- Pinch of ground black pepper
- ¼ cup mayonnaise
- 1/8 teaspoon Italian seasoning
- Pinch of garlic powder

SERVINGS: 2

COOKING TIME: 8 MINUTES

HOW TO MAKE IT

1. Preheat a mini waffle iron and grease it.
2. For the chaffles: Put all the ingredients in a medium bowl and with a fork, mix until well combined.
3. Put half of the mixture in the preheated waffle iron and cook for about 3-4 minutes.
4. Continue with the rest of the batter.
5. In the mean time, for the dip: in a bowl, mix together the cream and stevia.
6. Serve the waffles hot along with the dip.

NUTRITION

Calories 248, Sugar 0.2 g, Net Carbs 1.2 g, Total Fat 24.3 g, Cholesterol 98 mg, Protein 5.9 g, Saturated Fat 4.9 g, Sodium 374 mg, Total Carbs 1.g, Fiber 0.4 g

- -

SHIRATAKI RICE CHAFFLE

INGREDIENTS

- 2 eggs (beaten)
- 2 tbsp almond flour
- 1 cup shredded cheddar cheese
- 1 tsp baking powder
- 1 bag of shirataki rice
- ½ tsp oregano

SERVINGS: 4

COOKING TIME: 20 MINUTES

HOW TO MAKE IT

1. Wash the shirataki rice with warm water for about 30 seconds and then rinse it.
2. Switch on the waffle iron to preheat it and spray it with non-stick cooking spray.
3. Combine the rinsed rice, almond flour, baking powder, oregano and grated cheese in a bowl. Mix in the eggs until the ingredients are well combined. Stuff the waffle iron with an adequate amount of the batter and spread it to the edges to cover all the holes in the waffle iron.
4. Shut the waffle iron and cook for a few minutes or according to the settings on your waffle iron. After the cooking cycle is complete, use a silicone or plastic utensil to take the waffles out of the waffle maker.
5. Repeat steps 4 through 6 until you have cooked all the batter in the waffles.
6. Serve and enjoy!

NUTRITION

Carbohydrate 2g 1%, Fat 13.2g 17%, Sugars 0.3g, Protein 10.6g. 238 k

CORNBREAD JALAPENO CHAFFLE

INGREDIENTS

- 1 large egg beaten
- 2 tsp natural sweetener sweetener
- 1 small jalapeno (seeded and sliced)
- 3 tbsp almond flour
- ½ tsp all spice
- 1 milliliter cornbread flavoring
- 2 tbsp Mexican blend cheese
- 2 tbsp shredded parmesan cheese
- 1 ½ tbsp melted butter

NUTRITION

Carbohydrate 4.1g 1%, Fat 13.6g 17%, Sugars 0.8g, Protein 6.4g, 268 kcal

  SERVINGS: 3

COOKING TIME: 12 MINUTES

HOW TO MAKE IT

1. Insert the waffle iron to preheat it and mist it with non-stick spray.
2. Combine the almond flour, spices, jalapeño, baking powder and natural sweetener in a bowl.
3. In another bowl, whisk together the butter, egg and cornbread flavoring.
4. Stir the egg mixture into the flour mixture and blend until a soft dough forms. Add the cheese.
5. Spread a little Parmesan cheese on top of the chaffle iron.
6. Pour some of the batter into the waffle iron and spread the batter to the edges in order to cover all the holes in the waffle maker.
7. Spread a little Parmesan on top of the batter.
8. Close the waffle maker and bake for approximately 5 minutes or according to the settings on your waffle iron.
9. When baking cycle is complete, remove waffles from waffle iron with a plastic or silicone utensil.
10. Continue steps 5 to 7 until you have cooked all the batter in the waffles.
11. Serve them hot with the desired topping and enjoy them!

EGGS BENEDICT CHAFFLE

INGREDIENTS

- For the chaffle:
- 1 Tbsp sour cream
- 2 egg whites
- ½ cup mozzarella cheese
- 2 Tbsp almond flour
- For the hollandaise:
- 2 Tbsp lemon juice
- ½ cup salted butter
- 4 egg yolks
- For the poached eggs:
- 3 oz deli ham
- 2 eggs
- 1 Tbsp white vinegar

HOW TO MAKE IT

1. Beat the egg white until frothy and then mix in the rest of the ingredients.
2. Put the waffle iron to warm up and grease it with cooking spray. Cook for 7 minutes until golden brown.
3. Take out the waffles and repeat the operation with the rest of the batter.
4. Half fill the pan with water and boil.
5. Put a heatproof bowl on top of the pan, making sure the bottom does not touch the boiling water. Heat the butter to boiling point in the microwave. Stir the egg yolks into the bowl of the bain-marie and bring to a boil.
6. Pour the hot butter into the bowl and whisk vigorously.
7. Cook until the yolk mixture has thickened. Remove the bowl from the saucepan and pour in the lemon juice. Set aside. A
8. dd more water to the pot if necessary to cook the poached eggs (the water should completely cover the eggs).
9. Add the white vinegar to the water.

10. Crack the eggs into the boiling water and cook for 1 minute and 30 seconds. Remove with a skimmer.
11. Heat the chaffle in the toaster for 2-3 minutes. Top with ham, poached eggs and hollandaise sauce.
12. Serve and enjoy!

SERVINGS: 2

COOKING TIME: 10 MINUTES

AROMATIC OREGANO CHAFFLES

INGREDIENTS

- 2 Tbsp almond flour
- 1 medium egg
- ½ tsp oregano
- ½ cup mozzarella cheese, grated
- ½ tsp salt
- ½ tsp garlic powder
- For the toppings:
- ½ tsp garlic powder
- 2 Tbsp butter, unsalted softened
- 2 tsp dried oregano for sprinkling
- ¼ cup grated mozzarella cheese

HOW TO MAKE IT

1. Heat the waffle iron and grease it with cooking spray.
2. In a bowl, beat the egg. Stir in the mozzarella, garlic powder, flour, oregano and salt, and mix.
3. Transfer half of the batter into the waffle iron.
4. Shut and cook for a few minutes. Remove the cooked waffles.
5. Continue with the rest of the batter.
6. Place the waffles on a tray and preheat the grill.
7. Combine the butter with the garlic powder and spread it over the waffles.
8. Spread the mozzarella on top and cook under the grill for 2-3 minutes, until the cheese has melted.

NUTRITION

Carbs: 1 g, Fat: 7 g, Protein: 4 g, Calories: 274.

SAUSAGE & VEGGIES CHAFFLES

INGREDIENTS

- 2 tablespoons Mozzarella cheese, shredded
- 4 medium organic eggs
- 2 tablespoons bell peppers, seeded and chopped
- 2 tablespoons gluten-free breakfast sausage, cut into slices
- 2 tablespoons broccoli florets, chopped
- 1/3 cup unsweetened almond milk

HOW TO MAKE IT

I. Preheat a waffle iron and grease it. Mix almond milk and eggs in a bowl and whisk well.

2. Add tall the remaining ingredients and stir to combine well.

3. Put ¼ of the mixture in the preheated waffle iron and cook for about 5 minutes or until golden brown.

4. Repeat with the rest of the mixture. Serve hot and enjoy!

  SERVINGS: 4

COOKING TIME: 20 MINUTES

NUTRITION

Calories: 232, Net Carb: 1.2g, Sugar: 0.5gFat: 9.2g, Saturated Fat: 3.5g, Protein: 11.1g, Carbohydrates: 1.4g, Dietary Fiber: 0.2g.

....

CHEESY SALMON CHAFFLE

INGREDIENTS

Chaffles
- 2 eggs
- ½ ounce butter, melted
- 2 tbsp almond flour
- 1 cup mozzarella cheese, shredded
- Salt to taste

Filling
- 1/3 cup avocado, sliced
- ½ cup smoked salmon
- 2 tbsp feta cheese, crumbled

HOW TO MAKE IT

I. Preheat your waffle maker and make sure it is well greased.

2. In a bowl, place all ingredients and whisk until everything is well combined. Place ¼ of the mixture into preheated waffle maker and cook it for about 5-6 minutes. Repeat with the rest of the mixture.

3. Let them cool down for few minutes and garnish with your sliced avocado and smoked salmon. Sprinkles the fat cheese on top. Serve each and enjoy!

  SERVINGS: 4

COOKING TIME: 24 MINUTES

NUTRITION

Calories 269 Net Carbs 1.2 g Total Fat 13.g Saturated Fat 5 g Cholesterol 101 mg Sodium 319 mg Total Carbs 2.8 g Fiber 1.6 g Sugar 0.6 g Protein 8.9 g

CAULIFLOWER LOVE CHAFFLE

INGREDIENTS

- 1 egg
- 1/2 cup cauliflower
- 1/2 cup shredded cheddar cheese
- 1/4 tsp. garlic powder
- 1/4 tsp. black pepper
- 1/4 tsp. salt

For topping:

- 1 tomato sliced
- 1 lettuce leave
- 4 oz. cauliflower steamed, mashed
- 1 tsp sesame seeds

SERVINGS: 2

COOKING TIME: 15 MINUTES

HOW TO MAKE IT

1. Mix all chaffle ingredients into a blender and blend them thoroughly.
2. Sprinkle 1/8 shredded cheese on the waffle maker and pour cauliflower mixture in a preheated waffle maker and spatter the rest of the cheese over it.
3. Cook the chaffles for about 4-5 minutes until cooked. Serve with lettuce leaves over on top with steamed cauliflower and tomato slices.
4. Drizzle sesame seeds on top and enjoy!

NUTRITION

Protein: 25% 249 kcal Fat: 65% 128 kcal Carbohydrates: 10% 21 kcal

PULLED PORK COLESLAW CHAFFLE SANDWICH

INGREDIENTS

- 2 eggs, beaten
- 2 cups cooked and shredded pork
- 2 cups shredded coleslaw mix
- 1 cup finely grated cheddar cheese
- 1 tbsp sugar-free BBQ sauce
- 2 tbsp apple cider vinegar
- ¼ tsp baking powder
- ¼ cup ranch dressing
- ½ tsp salt
- pinch of pepper

SERVINGS: 4

COOKING TIME: 28 MINUTES

HOW TO MAKE IT

1. Preheat the waffle iron. In a medium bowl, mix the pulled pork with the BBQ sauce until well combined and set it aside.
2. Mix also the coleslaw mix, apple cider vinegar, salt, and ranch dressing in another bowl.
3. Mix the eggs in a medium bowl with cheddar cheese, and baking powder.
4. Add a quarter of the mixture in the maker, close and cook for 7 minutes until crispy.
5. Make 3 more chaffles in the same way.
6. When the chaffles are ready divide the pork in two and top with the ranch coleslaw and a pinch of pepper.
7. Cover with the remaining chaffles and insert mini skewers to secure the sandwiches.
8. Enjoy!

NUTRITION

Calories 374, Fats 23.61g, Carbs 8.2g, Net Carbs 8.2g, Protein 28.05g

BACON & JALAPENO CHAFFLE

INGREDIENTS

- 1 large egg
- 1 oz. cream cheese
- 2 tbsp bacon bits
- 1/2 cup cheddar cheese
- 1/2 tbsp jalapenos
- 1/4 tsp baking powder

HOW TO MAKE IT

1. Prepare your waffle maker. Grease it with cooking spray and let it warm. Blend in a bowl egg and vanilla extract together.
2. Add bacon bites, jalapenos, and baking powder.
3. Last, add in cheese and mix all together.
4. Pour the chaffles batter into the maker and cook it for about 2-3 minutes. When the chaffle is ready, remove it from the maker.
5. Enjoy it hot!

 SERVINGS:2

 COOKING TIME: 5 MINUTES

NUTRITION

Protein: 24% 295 kcal, Fat: 70% 175 kcal, Carbohydrates: 6% 15 kcal

---

ITALIAN FLAG SANDWICH CHAFFLES

INGREDIENTS

Chaffles
- 1 large organic egg, beaten
- ½ cup cheese, shredded
- 1/8 tsp vanilla drops

Filling
- 1 organic tomato, sliced finely
- Fresh Mozzarella, sliced
- fresh basil leaves

HOW TO MAKE IT

1. Preheat a mini waffle maker and oil it.
2. For the waffles: in a small bowl, place all the ingredients and give them a good mix.
3. Place half the mixture in the preheated waffle maker and cook for few minutes until golden brown.
4. Repeat with the rest of the batter.
5. Place each waffle in a plate with three tomato slices and three mozzarella slices alternating the two of them. Ad two basil leaves. Enjoy!

 SERVINGS: 2

 COOKING TIME: 6 MINUTES

NUTRITION

Calories 255 Net Carbs 2.4 g Total Fat 11.g Saturated Fat 6.8 g Cholesterol 118 mg Sodium 217 mg Total Carbs 3 g Fiber 0.6 g Sugar 1.4 g Protein 9.6 g

PORK & TOMATO SANDWICH CHAFFLES

INGREDIENTS

Chaffles

- 2 ground eggs
- ¼ cup fine almond flour
- ½ tsp garlic powder
- 1 cup cheddar cheese, shredded
- ¾ tsp baking powder

Filling

- 12 ounces pre cooked pork, sliced
- 1 tomato, sliced
- Lettuce leaves

SERVINGS: 4

COOKING TIME: 16 MINUTES

HOW TO MAKE IT

1. Preheat a mini waffle maker and oil it.
2. For the waffles:
3. In a bowl, combine the eggs, baking powder, flour and garlic powder and stir until everything results well mixed. Add the cheese and mix to blend it all together.
4. Place ¼ of the mixture in the preheated waffle maker and cook for about 3 minutes.
5. Repeat with the rest of the batter. Serve each waffle with the topping ingredients.

NUTRITION

Calories 319   Net Carbs 2.5 g Total Fat 18.2 g Saturated Fat 8 g Cholesterol 185 mg Sodium 263 mg Total Carbs 3.5 g Fiber 1 g Sugar 0.9 g Protein 34.2 g

TASTY TUNA SANDWICH CHAFFLES

INGREDIENTS

Chaffles

- 1 organic egg, beaten
- ½ cup cheddar cheese, shredded
- Salt to taste
- 1 tbsp almond flour

Filling

- 2 lettuce leaves
- ¼ cup water-packed tuna, flaked

SERVINGS: 2

COOKING TIME: 8 MINUTES

HOW TO MAKE IT

1. Preheat a mini waffle maker and coat it with oil.
2. For the waffles: In a medium mixing bowl, combine all the ingredients and whisk with a fork until they are well combined.
3. Put half of the combination into the preheated waffle maker and allow to cook for about 3-4 minutes. Do the same with the remaining mixture.
4. Now serve each waffle with the topping ingredients.

NUTRITION

Calories 286 Net Carbs 0.9 g Total Fat 13.6 g Saturated Fat 6.8 g Cholesterol 120 mg Sodium 342 mg Total Carbs 1.3 g Fiber 0.4 g Sugar 0.g Protein 13.6 g

FRIED EGGS AND GRUYERE CHAFFLES

INGREDIENTS

- 2 tbsp finely grated cheddar cheese
- 1 cup finely grated Gruyere cheese
- 2 eggs beaten
- 2 sunshine fried eggs for topping
- 3 tbsp minced fresh chives + more for garnishing
- 1/8 tsp. black pepper

HOW TO MAKE IT

1. Heat the waffle iron. In a medium bowl, mix cheeses, eggs, black pepper and chives.
2. Turn the iron on and spread half of the mixture.
3. Shut the iron and cook until golden brown and crisp, for about 7 minutes. T
4. ransfer the chaffle to a plate and set aside.
5. Prepare another chaffle with the remaining mixture.
6. Cover each chaffle with a fried egg, garnish with the chives and serve.
7. Serve and enjoy!

 SERVINGS: 2

COOKING TIME: 14 MINUTES

NUTRITION

Calories 512, Carbs 3.g, Net Carbs 3.78g, Protein 23.75g, Fats 41.32g.

SWISS CHEESE AND BACON CHAFFLE

INGREDIENTS

- ½ cup Swiss cheese
- 2 tbsp. cooked crumbled bacon
- 1 egg

HOW TO MAKE IT

1. Warm up your waffle iron.
2. Mix the egg in a bowl. Stir in bacon and cheese.
3. Transfer half of the mixture into the appliance. Seal and cook for minutes.
4. Make the second waffle following the same steps.
5. Serve and enjoy!

 SERVINGS: 2

COOKING TIME: 8 MINUTES

NUTRITION

Calories 223, Saturated Fat 8.1g, Sugars 0.5g, Fat 17.6g Sodium 522mg

Carbohydrate 1.9g Fiber 0g Cholesterol 128mg Protein 17.1g

OLIVES AND BACON CHAFFLE

INGREDIENTS

- ½ cup cheddar cheese, shredded
- 1 tbsp. black olives, chopped
- 1 egg
- 1 tbsp. bacon bits ½ cup cheddar cheese, shredded
- 1 tbsp. black olives, chopped
- 1 egg
- 1 tbsp. bacon bits

HOW TO MAKE IT

1. Turn on your waffle iron and pre-heat. Stir the egg and mix in the cheese in a bowl.
2. Add in the black olives and the bacon bites and mix well. Pour half of the obtained mixture into the waffle iron.
3. Cook for 4 minutes or until golden.
4. Remove and let it cool for 2 minutes. Repeat the procedure to make another waffle.
5. Enjoy!

SERVINGS: 2
COOKING TIME: 8 MINUTES

NUTRITION

Calories 202, Protein 13.4g Total Fat 16g Saturated Fat 8g Total Carbohydrate 0.9g Potassium 111mg Cholesterol 122mg Total Sugars 0.3g Sodium 462mg Dietary Fiber 0.1g

---

BASIL NUT PUMPKIN CHAFFLE

INGREDIENTS

- 1/4 tsp pumpkin pie spice
- 1 egg
- 2 tbsp Basil Nut, toasted and chopped
- 1/2 cup mozzarella cheese, grated
- 1 tsp erythritol
- 1 tbsp pumpkin puree
- 2 tbsp almond flour.

HOW TO MAKE IT

1. Warm up the waffle iron. Crack the egg in a small bowl. Put together the rest of the ingredients and mix well.
2. Mist the waffle iron with cooking spray.
3. Add half of the batter into the hot waffle iron and cook for a few minutes or until golden brown.
4. Do the same with the rest of the batter.
5. Serve and enjoy!

SERVINGS: 2
COOKING TIME: 8 MINUTES

NUTRITION

Calories 221, Carbohydrates 5.7g, Sugar 3.3g, Fat 9.g, Protein 6.7g, Cholesterol 86 mg.

PUMPKIN NUTTY CHAFFLE

INGREDIENTS

- 1 egg, beaten
- 2 tablespoons almond flour
- ½ cup mozzarella cheese, grated
- ½ teaspoon pumpkin spice
- 2 tablespoons pecans, chopped
- 2 tablespoons peanuts, chopped
- 1 tablespoon pureed pumpkin
- 1 teaspoon sweetener
- maple syrup

HOW TO MAKE IT

1. Turn on the waffle iron.
2. Whip the egg in a bowl, mix in the rest of the ingredients. Pour in your maker half of the mixture.
3. Close the lid and cook for 5 minutes.
4. When ready lift the chaffle carefully.
5. Repeat the above steps to make the other chaffle.
6. Top with peanuts and pecans and maple syrup at your taste.

SERVINGS: 2

COOKING TIME: 8 MINUTES

NUTRITION

Calories 210, Total Fat 17 g, Saturated Fat 10 g, Cholesterol 110mg, Sodium 250 mg, Potassium 570 mg, Total Carbohydrate 4.6 g, Dietary Fiber 1.7 g, Protein 11 g, Total Sugars 2 g

BASIC COCONUT CHAFFLES

INGREDIENTS

- 1 cup mozzarella
- 1 tbsp. coconut oil
- 1 tsp baking powder
- 1 egg
- ¼ cup almond flour

HOW TO MAKE IT

1. Preheat your non-stick pan over medium heat.
2. Combine all the ingredients in a bowl. Oil the pan with avocado oil and place a heart-shaped cookie cutter on the pan.
3. Pour the batter evenly into 2 cookie cutters once the pan is hot.
4. Cook for another 1-2 minutes. As soon as the waffles are set, remove the cutters, flip over and cook for a further 1-2 minutes. Remove from the pan as soon as the chaffles are brown.
5. Serve hot and enjoy!

SERVINGS: 2

COOKING TIME: 5 MINUTES

NUTRITION

Protein: 24% 2243 kcal, Fat: 6 123 kcal, Carbohydrates: 6%

COCONUT CHOCOLATE BALLS ON CHAFFLES

INGREDIENTS

- 1/4 cup heavy cream
- ½ cup non-sweetened cocoa
- 1 egg
- 1/4 cup coconut flour
- ½ cup mozzarella cheese

HOW TO MAKE IT

1. Make 2 chaffles with chaffle ingredients as we learned.
2. Combine all the ingredients in a mixing bowl in the meantime. Use the mixture to form two balls and place in the freezer for at least 2 hours until firm.
3. Then serve your chafes with the chocolate ballsand.
4. Enjoy!

 SERVINGS: 2

 COOKING TIME: 5 MINUTES

NUTRITION

Protein: 18% 46 kcal Fat: 78% 196 kcal Carbohydrates: 4%

- -

MAYONNAISE & GARLIC CHAFFLES

INGREDIENTS

- 1 tbsp. chia seeds
- 2 ½ tbsps. water
- 2 tbsps. coconut flour
- ¼ cup low carb vegan cheese
- 1 cup low carb vegan cream cheese, softened
- Salt to taste
- 2 tbsps. vegan garlic mayo for topping
- 1 tsp. garlic powder

HOW TO MAKE IT

1. Preheat your waffle maker.
2. In a small bowl, stir together the chia seeds and water and let sit for 5 minutes.
3. Add all ingredients to the chia seed batter and blend well.
4. Place the vegan batter in a lightly greased waffle maker.
5. Close the lid and cook for approximately 3 minutes.
6. Once the waffles are done, they should be removed from the waffle maker. Garnish with garlic mayonnaise and pepper.
7. Enjoy!

 SERVINGS: 2

 COOKING TIME: 5 MINUTES

NUTRITION

Protein: 32% 242 kcal Fat: 63% 82 kcal Carbohydrates: 5%

FRUITY VEGAN CHAFFLES

INGREDIENTS

- 1 tbsp. chia seeds
- 2 tbsps. warm water
- ¼ cup low carb vegan cheese
- 2 tbsps. strawberry puree
- 2 tbsps. Greek yogurt pinch of salt

NUTRITION

Protein: 32%, 242 kcal Fat: 63%
Carbohydrates: 5%

HOW TO MAKE IT

1. Pre-heat waffle maker to medium-high heat.
2. Mix together chia seeds and water in a small bowl, and let it stand for few minutes to be thickened. Mix the rest of the ingredients in chia seed egg and mix well.
3. Spray waffle machine with cooking spray. Pour vegan waffle batter into the center of the waffle iron. Close the waffle maker and cook for about 3-5 minutes.
4. Once cooked, remove from the maker and serve with berries on top.

 SERVINGS:2

 COOKING TIME:5MINUTES

TINY CHAFFLE BITES

INGREDIENTS

- 6 tsp coconut flour
- 3 oz. cream cheese
- 1/2. tsp vanilla extract
- 1 tsp stevia
- 1/4 tsp baking powder
- 2 eggs
- Topping:
- 1 egg
- 6 slice bacon
- 2 oz. Raspberries for topping
- 2 oz. Blueberries for topping
- 2 oz. Strawberries for topping

HOW TO MAKE IT

1. Pre-heat your wonderful waffle maker and grease with cooking spray.
2. Mix together coconut flour, stevia, baking powder, egg, cheese and vanilla in a mixing bowl.
3. Pour ½ of chaffles mixture in a waffle maker.
4. Secure the lid and cook the chaffles for about 3-5 minutes.
5. Meantime, fry bacon slices in pan on medium heat for about 2-3 minutes until cooked and transfer them to plate.
6. In the same pan, fry eggs one by one in the leftover grease of bacon.
7. Once chaffles are cooked, carefully transfer them to the plate.
8. Serve with fried eggs and bacon slice and berries on top and enjoy!

 SERVINGS: 3

COOKING TIME: 15 MINUTES

NUTRITION

per Servings: Protein: 346 kcal; 16%; 75 kcal Fat: 75%; Carbohydrates: 9%

ITALIAN BRUSCHETTA CHAFFLE

INGREDIENTS

- 1 tomato sliced
- 1 tablespoon olives, sliced
- 2 basic chaffles
- Basil leaves
- 1 tablespoon keto friendly pesto sauce
- 2 tablespoons mozzarella, shredded
- 2 tablespoons sugar-free marinara sauce

HOW TO MAKE IT

1. Coat each chamfer with marinara sauce.
2. Spread pesto over marinara sauce with a spoon. Cover with tomato, olives and mozzarella.
3. Oven for 3 minutes or until cheese melts down.
4. Top with basil.
5. Serve and enjoy!

 SERVINGS: 2

 COOKING TIME: 5 MINUTES

NUTRITION

Calories 182, Total Fat 11g, Dietary Fiber 1.1g, Saturated Fat 6.1g, Potassium 1 mg, Cholesterol 30mg, Total Carbohydrate 3.1g, Sodium 508 mg, Protein 16.8g, Total Sugars 1g.

SWEET BANANA CHAFFLE

INGREDIENTS

- ½ tsp banana flavoring
- 1/8 tsp salt
- 2 tbsp almond flour
- ½ shredded mozzarella cheese
- 2 eggs (beaten)
- ½ tsp baking powder
- ½ tsp cinnamon
- 2 tbsp natural sweetener sweetener

HOW TO MAKE IT

1. Plug the waffle maker to preheat it and spray it with a non-stick spray.
2. In a mixing bowl, combine the baking flour, cinnamon, natural sweetener, salt, almond flour and cheese. Add the egg and banana flavor.
3. Mix until the ingredients are well combined. Pour ¼ of the batter into your waffle maker and spread out the batter to cover all the holes on the waffle maker.
4. Close the waffle maker and cook for about minutes or according to your waffle maker's settings.
5. After the cooking cycle, use a silicone or plastic utensil to take out the chaffle from the waffle iron.
6. Repeat step 3 to 5 until you have cooked all the batter into chaffles.
7. Serve warm and enjoy!

 SERVINGS: 4

 COOKING TIME: 16 MINUTES

NUTRITION

Fat 12.5g 16% Carbohydrate 11g 7% Sugars 0.7g Protein 8.8g, 268 kcal

47

DELICIOUS APPLE CHAFFLE

INGREDIENTS

- 1/3 cup mozzarella cheese
- 1 tsp cinnamon
- 1 tbsp almond flour
- 1 big apple (finely chopped)
- 1 tbsp heavy whipping cream
- 1 egg beaten
- ½ tsp vanilla extract
- 1 tbsp granulated natural sweetener
- ¼ tbsp sugar free maple syrup

SERVINGS: 2

COOKING TIME: 6 MINUTES

HOW TO MAKE IT

1. Switch on the chaffle maker and preheat it. Spray with non-stick spray.
2. Combine the natural sweetener, almond flour, mozzarella, cinnamon and chopped apple in a large bowl.
3. Mix in the eggs, vanilla extract and whipping cream. Stir until everything is well combined.
4. Pour the batter into the chaffle maker and spread the batter to the edges of the waffle iron to all the wells of the waffle iron. Shut the lid of the waffle iron and cook for about 5 minutes or according to the settings of the waffle iron.
5. After the cooking cycle is complete, remove the waffles from the waffle iron with a plastic or silicone utensil.
6. Continue steps 4 to 6 until you have cooked all the batter in the waffles. Serve and top up with some maple syrup.
7. Don't exceed with sugars!

NUTRITION

Sugars 12.1g, Fat 7.8g 10%, Carbohydrate 1g 7%, Protein 5.4g, 268 kcal

---

PEANUT BUTTER AND CHOCOLATE CHIPS

INGREDIENTS

- For filling:
- 3 tbsp creamy peanut butter
- 2 tbsp natural sweetener
- 1 tbsp butter, softened
- For chaffle:
- 1 tbsp natural sweetener
- 1 tbsp unsweetened chocolate chips
- 1/2 cup mozzarella cheese, shredded
- 2 tbsp cocoa powder
- 1/4 tsp espresso powder
- 1 egg, lightly beaten

SERVINGS: 1

COOKING TIME: 15 MINUTES

HOW TO MAKE IT

1. Preheat the waffle iron. In a bowl, blend the egg, espresso powder, chocolate chips, natural sweetener and cocoa powder.
2. Mix in the mozzarella cheese and stir well.
3. Mist the waffle maker with cooking spray.
4. Place 1/2 of the batter in the hot waffle iron and cook for 3-4 minutes or until golden brown.
5. Continue with the rest of the batter.
6. For the filling: combine butter, natural sweetener and peanut butter until smooth in a small bowl.
7. When the chaffles are cool, spread the filling mixture between two chaffles and let them rest for 10 minutes in the fridge.
8. Cut the chaffle sandwich in half and serve.

NUTRITION

Calories 300, Protein 8.2g, Carbohydrates 9.6 g, Fat 16.1 g, Sugar 1.1 g, Cholesterol 101 mg.

CHOCOLATE CHIPS CHAFFLE ROLLS

INGREDIENTS

- 1 tsp stevia
- 1 egg
- 1 tsp cinnamon
- 1 tbsp. almond flour
- 1/2 cup mozzarella cheese
- TOPPING:
- 1 tbsp. coconut flour
- 1/4 cup keto chocolate chips
- 1 tbsp. coconut cream

HOW TO MAKE IT

1. Turn on your (round) waffle iron and let it warm up.
2. Mix together the cheese, egg, flour, cinnamon powder and stevia in a small bowl.
3. Mist the waffle iron with nonstick spray.
4. Pour the batter into the waffle iron and cook for about 3-4 minutes.
5. After the waffles are cooked to your liking, carefully remove them from the maker. In the meantime, mix the cream flour and chocolate chips in a bowl and heal in the microwave for it to amalgamate for 30 seconds.
6. Roll up the waffles and spread this filling over the waffles and roll them up.
7. Enjoy!

 SERVINGS: 2

 COOKING TIME: 10 MINUTES

NUTRITION

Carbohydrates: 7%, Protein: 32% 250 kcal, Fat: 61%

VEGAN CHOCOLATE CHAFFLES

INGREDIENTS

- 1/2 cupcoconut flour
- 3 tbsps. cocoa powder
- 2 tbsps. whole psyllium husk
- 1/2 teaspoon baking powder
- 1/2 cup vegan cheese, softened
- 1/4 cup coconut milk
- pinch of salt

HOW TO MAKE IT

1. Prepare your waffle iron according to the manufacturer's instructions.
2. Mix together coconut flour, cocoa powder, baking powder, salt and husk in a bowl and set aside.
3. Add melted cheese and milk and mix well. Let it stand for a few minutesutes before cooking.
4. Pour batter in waffle machine and cook for about 3-minutesutes.
5. Once chaffles are cooked, carefully remove them from the waffle machine.
6. Serve with vegan icecream and enjoy!

 SERVINGS:2

 COOKING TIME:5MINUTES

NUTRITION

Protein: 32% 242 kcal Fat: 63% 82 kcal Carbohydrates: 5%

FLAXSEED CHAFFLE

INGREDIENTS

- 1 tbsp. flaxseed meal
- 2 tbsps. warm water
- ¼ cup low carb vegan cheese
- ¼ cup chopped minutest pinch of salt
- 2 oz. blueberries chunks

NUTRITION

Protein: 34% 292 kcal Fat: 68%

Carbohydrates: 5%

HOW TO MAKE IT

1. Prepare the waffle maker on medium-high heat and coat with co-oking spray.
2. Blend together the flaxseed meal and warm water and put aside to allow them to thicken.
3. After 5 minutes whisk all the ingredients into the flaxseed mixture.
4. Pour the vegan waffle batter into the centre of the waffle maker.
5. Close the lid and leave to bake for 3 minutes. When cooked, remo-ve the waffle and enjoy!

  SERVINGS:2

COOKING TIME:5MINUTES

....

HALF MOON ICE CREAM CHAFFLE

INGREDIENTS

- 1 egg, beaten
- ½ cup finely grated mozzarella cheese
- ¼ cup almond flour
- 2 tbsp natural sweetener
- 1/8 tsp xanthan gum
- Low-carb ice cream (flavor of your choice) for serving

HOW TO MAKE IT

1. Preheat the waffle iron. Mix all the ingredients in a bowl (not the ice cream).
2. Add half of the mixture to the waffle maker, close it and cook until crispy for 7 minutes. Transfer the chaffle to a plate and make a se-cond one with the other half of the ingredients.
3. Add a scoop of you favorite low carb ice cream on each chaffle, fold into half-moons and enjoy.

  SERVINGS: 2

COOKING TIME: 14 MINUTES

NUTRITION

Calories 89, Fats 248g, Carbs 1.67g, Net Carbs 1.37g, Protein 5.91g

PEANUT BUTTER BLUEBERRY CHAFFLES

INGREDIENTS

- 1 egg
- ½ cup cheddar cheese, shredded
- Filling
- 1 tbsp butter, melted
- 2 tbsp erythritol or 1 tsp natural sweetener
- 2 tbsp cream cheese, softened
- 1 tbsp natural peanut butter
- ¼ tsp vanilla drops
- Blueberries

SERVINGS: 2

COOKING TIME: 10 MINUTES

HOW TO MAKE IT

1. Preheat your mini waffle maker and oil it.
2. In a bowl, mix the egg and the cheese. Combine the two ingredients well.
3. Place half of the mixture into preheated waffle maker. Cook your first chaffle.
4. Repeat with the rest of the mixture.
5. For filling: In a medium bowl, put all ingredients and whisk until everything is well combined.
6. Serve each chaffle with your peanut butter sauce.

NUTRITION

Calories 143   Net Carbs 3.3 g Total Fat 10.1 g Saturated Fat 4.5 g Cholesterol 100 mg Sodium 148 mg Total Carbs 4.1 g Fiber 0.8 g Sugar 1.2 g Protein 6 g

CREEMY GINGERBREAD CHAFFLE

INGREDIENTS

- 2 tbsp almond flour
- 1/8 tsp garlic powder
- ½ tsp baking powder
- ½ tsp cinnamon
- ½ cup mozzarella cheese
- 2 tsp natural sweetener
- 1 egg (beaten)
- ¼ tsp nutmeg
- ½ tsp ginger

Topping:

- 1 tsp cinnamon
- ½ cup heavy cream

SERVINGS: 2

COOKING TIME: 8 MINUTES

HOW TO MAKE IT

1. Connect the waffle iron to preheat and spray with non-stick cooking spray.
2. Combine the almond flour, baking powder, cinnamon, garlic, ginger, nutmeg, natural sweetener and cheese in a medium mixing bowl.
3. Include the egg and mix until the ingredients are combined.
4. Add an appropriate amount of batter to the waffle iron and distribute the batter to the edges to cover all the holes in the waffle iron. Shut the waffle iron and bake the waffles for about minutes or depending on the settings of your waffle iron.
5. Use a plastic or silicone utensil to remove the waffles from the waffle iron after cooking. Keep repeating steps 2 to 5 until you have baked all the batter into waffles.
6. Let the waffles cool for a few minutes. To make the filling, in a mixing bowl blend the heavy cream, cinnamon and syrup.
7. Mix until smooth and fluffy.
8. Coat the waffles with the cream mixture and serve.

NUTRITION

Fat 18.2g 23%, Carbohydrate 6.8g 2%, Sugars 0.6g, Protein 7g, kcal 301

COCONUT CHAFFLE STICKS

INGREDIENTS

- ¼ cup coconut flour
- 2 tablespoons powdered erythritol
- 2 cups mozzarella cheese, shredded
- 6 organic eggs
- 1 teaspoon ground cinnamon

NUTRITION

Calories 296, Net Carbs 1.5 g,
Total Fat 6.3 g, Saturated Fat 2.9
g, Cholesterol 130 mg, Sodium 99
mg, Total Carbs 3.2 g, Fiber 1.7 g,
Sugar 0.3 g, Protein 6.7 g.

SERVINGS: 8

COOKING TIME: 40 MINUTES

HOW TO MAKE IT

1. Heat your oven to 350°F and line a large baking sheet with a greased piece of foil.
2. Now preheat a waffle iron and grease it.
3. Put 4 eggs in a bowl and beat them well.
4. Next, add the cheese, coconut flour, erythritol and ½ teaspoon of cinnamon and blend until well mixed.
5. Add ¼ of the mixture to the preheated waffle iron and cook for approximately 6-8 minutes.
6. Then repeat the process with the remaining mixture.
7. Put the waffles aside to cool. Slice each waffle into 4 strips.
8. In a medium bowl, add the remaining eggs and cinnamon and beat well to blend.
9. Tip the spinner sticks evenly into the egg mixture.
10. Divide the sticks in a single layer on the prepared baking tray.
11. Cook for about 10 minutes. T
12. ake the baking tray out of the oven and brush the top of each chopstick with the melted butter.
13. Flip the sticks over and cook for about 6-8 minutes.
14. Serve immediately.

BLUEBERRY PEANUT BUTTER CHAFFLES

INGREDIENTS

- ½ cup cheddar cheese, shredded
- 1 organic egg

Filling

- 2 tsp fresh blueberries
- 1 tbsp natural peanut butter
- 2 tbsp cream cheese, softened
- 2 tbsp erythritol
- ¼ tsp organic vanilla extract
- 1 tbsp butter, softened

SERVINGS: 2

COOKING TIME: 10 MINUTES

HOW TO MAKE IT

1. Warm up a mini waffle iron and then oil it.
2. For the waffles: Place the egg and cheddar cheese in a small bowl and stir together.
3. Add half of the mixture to the pre-heated waffle iron and bake for about 5 minutes.
4. Do the same with the rest of the mixture. In the meantime, start making the filling: Combine all the ingredients in a large bowl and mix until well mixed.
5. Top each waffle with the peanut butter mixture.

NUTRITION

Calories 143, Net Carbs 3.3 g, Total Fat 10.1 g, Saturated Fat 4.5 g, Cholesterol 100 mg, Sodium 148 mg, Total Carbs 4.1 g, Fiber 0.8 g, Sugar 1.2 g, Protein 6 g.

DELICIOUS CHOCO CHAFFLES

INGREDIENTS

Chaffles

- 1 teaspoon vanilla extract
- 1 teaspoons erythritol
- 2 tablespoons almond flour
- 1 organic egg, beaten
- 1 tablespoon cacao powder
- 1 ounce cream cheese, softened

Filling

- ¼ tsp organic vanilla extract
- ½ tablespoon cacao powder
- 2 tbsp cream cheese, softened
- 2 tablespoons erythritol

 SERVINGS: 2

 COOKING TIME: 10 MINUTES

HOW TO MAKE IT

1. Warm up a mini waffle iron and then grease it.
2. For the waffles: Place all the ingredients in a medium bowl and whisk with well a fork until well combined.
3. Add half of the mixture to the preheated waffle iron and cook for approximately 3-5 minutes.
4. Do the same with the rest of the mixture.
5. Meanwhile, prepare the filling: Combine all the ingredients in a medium bowl and use a hand mixer to blend until well combined.
6. Top each waffle with the chocolate mixture.

NUTRITION

Calories 292, Net Carb: 2g, Total Fat 16 g, Saturated Fat 7.6 g, Cholesterol 113 mg, Sodium 115 mg, Total Carbs 4.4 g, Fiber 1.9 g, Sugar 0.8 g, Protein 5.7 g.

WHIPPING PEANUT CREAM CHAFFLES

INGREDIENTS

- ¼ teaspoon peanut butter extract
- 2 tablespoons Erythritol
- ¼ teaspoon organic baking powder
- 1 tablespoon heavy whipping cream
- 2 tablespoons sugar-free peanut butter powder
- 1 organic egg, beaten

 SERVINGS: 2

COOKING TIME: 8 MINUTES

HOW TO MAKE IT

1. Prepare a mini waffle iron and then grease it.
2. In a medium-sized bowl, place all the ingredients and use a fork to mix them together until well combined.
3. Pour half of the mixture into the preheated waffle iron and cook for about 4 minutes or until they are golden brown.
4. Do the same with the rest of the mixture.
5. To serve warm.

NUTRITION

Calories:312, Net Carb:1g,Fat:6.9g, Saturated Fat: 2.7g, Carbohydrates: 3.7g, Dietary Fiber: 2.1g, Sugar: 0.2g, Protein: 10.9g.

CHAFFLE CANNOLO

INGREDIENTS

- For the chaffles:
- 1 large egg
- 1 egg yolk
- 1 cup Parmesan cheese, grated
- 3 tbsp butter, melted
- 1 tbsp natural sweetener
- 2 tbsp mozzarella cheese, grated
- For the cannoli filling:
- ½ cup ricotta cheese
- 1 tsp vanilla extract
- 2 tbsp natural sweetener sugar
- 2 tbsp unsweetened chocolate chips for garnishing

SERVINGS: 4

COOKING TIME: 28 MINUTES

HOW TO MAKE IT

1. Preheat the waffle maker.
2. Mix all the ingredients for the chaffles in a medium bowl.
3. Pour in the maker a quarter of the mixture, cover, and cook for 7 minutes until crispy.
4. Remove and make 3 more chaffle dividing the remaining batter.
5. In the meanwhile, whip the ricotta cheese, add the sugar until smooth, lastly mix in the vanilla.
6. On each chaffle, spread some of the filling and carefully wrap it over.
7. Garnish the creamy ends with some chocolate chips. Serve immediately and enjoy.

NUTRITION

Calories 308, Fats 25.05g, Carbs 5.17g, Net Carbs 5.17g, Protein 15.18g

---

SOFT CHOCOLATE CHAFFLE

INGREDIENTS

For the chaffles:
- 2 eggs, beaten
- 2 tbsp heavy cream
- 2 tbsp cream cheese, softened
- 2 tsp vanilla extract
- 1 tbsp coconut flour
- 3 tbsp cocoa powder
- ¼ cup finely Gruyere cheese
- A pinch of salt

For the chocolate sauce:
- 1/3 cup + 1 tbsp heavy cream
- 1 ½ oz unsweetened baking chocolate, chopped
- 1 ½ tsp vanilla extract
- 1 ½ tsp sugar-free maple syrup

HOW TO MAKE IT

1. Preheat the waffle iron. Mix all the ingredients for the chaffles in a medium bowl. Pour a quarter of the batter in the mixture, close and cook for 7 minutes until crispy. Repeat the procedure to make other 3 chaffle.
2. For the chocolate sauce, pour the heavy cream into a saucepan and simmer over low heat for 3 minutes.
3. Turn the heat off and add the chocolate.
4. Leave it alone melting for a few minutes, then stir until fully melted, 5 minutes. Mix in the vanilla extract and maple syrup.
5. Assemble the chaffles in layers with the chocolate sauce sandwiched in between.
6. Slice and serve immediately.

SERVINGS: 4

COOKING TIME: 36 MINUTES

NUTRITION

Calories 272, Fats 13.57g, Carbs 6.65g, Net Carbs 3.65g, Protein 5.76g

CACAO AND VANILLA CHAFFLES

INGREDIENTS

- Chaffles
- 1 organic egg, beaten
- 2 tbsp almond flour
- 1 tbsp cacao powder
- 1 ounce cream cheese, softened
- 2 tsp erythritol or 1 tsp natural sweetener
- 1 tsp organic vanilla extract
- Filling
- 2 tbsp cream cheese, softened
- 2 tbsp erythritol
- ½ tbsp cacao powder

SERVINGS: 2

COOKING TIME: 10 MINUTES

HOW TO MAKE IT

1. Preheat and grease your waffle maker.
2. For the waffles: In a large bowl, place all the ingredients and using a fork, beat until well combined. Put half of the batter into the preheated waffle maker and cook for about 3-5 minutes.
3. Repeat with the remaining mixture.
4. Meanwhile, for the filling: In a large bowl, place all the components and with a hand mixer, whisk until well combined.
5. Serve each chaffle with the chocolate mixture you just prepared, drizzle dark chocolate chips.

NUTRITION

Calories 292 Net Carb: g Total Fat 16 g Saturated Fat 7.6 g Cholesterol 113 mg Sodium 115 mg Total Carbs 4.4 g Fiber 1.9 g Sugar 0.8 g Protein 5.7 g

---

CHAFFLE CANNOLI (VARIATION)

INGREDIENTS

For the chaffles:
- 1 large egg
- 2 tbsp finely grated mozzarella cheese
- 3 tbsp butter, melted
- 1 cup finely grated cheddar cheese
- 1 egg yolk
- 1 tbsp natural sweetener

For the cannoli filling:
- 1 tsp vanilla extract
- ½ cup ricotta cheese
- 2 tbsp crushed pistachios for garnishing
- 2 tbsp natural sweetener

HOW TO MAKE IT

1. Preheat the waffle iron. In a medium bowl, mix all the ingredients for the waffles.
2. Open the iron, pour in a quarter of the batter, cover and cook until crisp, approximately 7 minutes.
3. Transfer the chaffle to a plate and make 3 more with the rest of the batter.
4. Meantime, for the cannoli filling: whisk together the ricotta cheese and powdered sugar until smooth.
5. Add the vanilla.
6. On each cannoli, spread a little of the filling and wrap.
7. Decorate the creamy ends with a few chocolate chips.
8. Serve at once.

SERVINGS: 4

COOKING TIME: 28 MINUTES

NUTRITION

Calories 308, Fats 25.05, Carbs 5.17g, Net Carbs 5.17g, Protein 15.18g.

VANILLA, CHOCOLATE AND LEMON CHAFFLE

INGREDIENTS

- 2 tsp almond flour
- 2 tsp natural sweetener
- 2 eggs, lightly beaten
- 1/2 tsp vanilla
- 1/2 tsp lemon extract
- 1 tbsp unsweetened chocolate chips
- 1/2 cup mozzarella cheese, shredded

HOW TO MAKE IT

1. Warm up your waffle iron. In a bowl, whisk together the eggs, vanilla, natural sweetener, lemon extract, cheese and almond flour. Mix in the chocolate chips and stir well. Mist the waffle iron with cooking spray.
2. Drop 1/2 of the batter into the hot waffle iron and cook for 4 minutes or until golden brown. Continue with the rest of the dough.
3. Serve and enjoy!

 SERVINGS: 2

 COOKING TIME: 15 MINUTES

NUTRITION

Calories 315, Protein 9 g, Carbohydrates 5.4 g, Fat 10.8 g, Sugar 0.7 g, Cholesterol 167 mg.

....

CREEMY COCONUT AND BERRIES CHAFFLES

INGREDIENTS

- 1 cup shredded cheese
- 2 tbsp coconut flour
- 4 large eggs
- 1 tsp stevia
- 2 tbsp coconut cream
- TOPPING:
- 4 oz. blueberries
- 2 oz. cherries
- 8 oz. raspberries
- 1 cup heavy cream

HOW TO MAKE IT

1. Form 4 thin round chaffles with the chaffle ingredients.
2. When the chaffles are cooked, layer them on a plate.
3. Top each layer with heavy cream. Cover with blueberries and then with raspberries and cherries.
4. Serve and enjoy!

 SERVINGS: 4

 COOKING TIME: 15 MINUTES

NUTRITION

230 kcal ,Protein: 21%, Fat: 72%

LEMONY CREEM CHAFFLE

INGREDIENTS

- 1/8 tsp salt
- 1 egg
- 2 tsp natural sweetener sweetener
- ½ lemon (juiced)
- ½ tsp lemon zest
- ¼ tsp baking powder
- 2 tbsp almond flour
- 2 tbsp cream cheese
- ½ apple (peeled and finely chopped)

Lemon Icing:

- 1 tsp freshly squeezed lemon juice

SERVINGS: 2

COOKING TIME: 12 MINUTES

HOW TO MAKE IT

1. Turn on the waffle iron to preheat it and spray it with non-stick cooking spray.
2. Mix the egg, lemon zest, cream cheese and lemon juice in a mixing bowl and mix the salt, natural sweetener, almond flour, baking powder and chopped apple together in another mixing bowl.
3. Add the egg mixture to the flour mixture and blend until the ingredients are mixed well together and you have formed a very smooth dough.
4. Add an adequate amount of batter to the waffle iron and distribute the batter to the edges to cover all the holes in the waffle iron.
5. Shut the waffle iron and bake until the waffles are browned.
6. Each waffle will take about 5 minutes to cook, but the cooking time may vary on some waffle irons. Use a silicone or plastic utensil to remove the waffles from the waffle iron after cooking.
7. Continue to repeat steps 5 to 7 until you have baked all the batter into waffles.
8. Mix the lemon juice, lemon zest, cream and icing sugar powder in a mixing bowl for the topping.
9. Blend well until the mixture results soft and fluffy.
10. Distribute the cream mixture over the chaffles and enjoy!

NUTRITION

Fat 12.1g 16%, Carbohydrate 14.2g 5%, Sugars 7.2g, Protein 5.5g, kcal 316

STRAWBERRY SHORTCAKE CHAFFLE

INGREDIENTS

- 1 egg (beaten)
- 2 tsp granulated natural sweetener
- ½ cup shredded mozzarella cheese
- 1 tbsp almond flour
- 1 tsp sugar free maple syrup
- ½ tsp cinnamon
- Topping:
- 4 tbsp cream cheese (softened)
- 1 tbsp heavy cream
- 3 fresh strawberries (sliced)
- ¼ tsp vanilla extract
- 2 tsp granulated natural sweetener

SERVINGS: 2

COOKING TIME: 8 MINUTES

HOW TO MAKE IT

1. Connect the waffle iron to preheat and spray with non-stick cooking spray.
2. Mix the cinnamon, natural sweetener, cheese and almond flour in a mixing bowl.
3. Next, add the egg and maple syrup. Mix until the ingredients are well incorporated.
4. Then pour an appropriate amount of the batter into the waffle iron and distribute the batter to the edges in order to cover all the holes in the waffle iron.
5. Shut the waffle iron and cook the waffles for around minutes or depending on the settings of your waffle iron.
6. When cooked, remove the waffles from the waffle iron using a plastic or silicone utensil.
7. Continue to repeat steps 3 to 5 until you have cooked all the batter into waffles.
8. To make the topping, mix the cream cheese, natural sweetener vanilla and cream in a mixing bowl.
9. Beat the mixture until it is smooth and fluffy. Place the cream and sliced strawberries on top of the chaffles.
10. Serve and enjoy!

NUTRITION

Fat 15g 19% Carbohydrate 5.2g 2% Sugars 1.3g Protein 7.3g, kcal 312

CHOCO COCO STRAWBERRY DELIGHT

INGREDIENTS

- 1 tsp. vanilla extract
- 1 cup coconut flour
- 1/4 cup coconut cream, frozen
- ¼ cup strawberries chunks
- 4 keto chaffles
- 1 oz. chocolate flakes

SERVINGS: 2

COOKING TIME: 5 MINUTES

HOW TO MAKE IT

1. This topping recipe is perfect for your leftover chaffles.
2. Combine the toppings ingredients in a bowl.
3. Divide the mixture between the chamfers and put in the freezer. Freeze for 2 hours.
4. Take your previously made or leftover chafes and garnish with the topping.
5. Serve cold and enjoy.

NUTRITION

Protein: 26%, Fat: 71%, Carbohydrates: 3% 319 kcal

PUMPKIN DOUBLE CREAM CHAFFLE

INGREDIENTS

- For chaffle:
- 1 egg
- 1 tbsp natural sweetener
- 1/4 tsp pumpkin spice
- 1/2 tsp baking powder, gluten-free
- 2 tsp heavy cream
- 1/2 tsp vanilla
- 2 tsp pumpkin puree
- 1 tsp cream cheese, softened
- 1/2 cup mozzarella cheese, shredded

SERVINGS: 2

COOKING TIME: 15 MINUTES

HOW TO MAKE IT

1. Preheat your waffle iron.
2. Combine all the chaffle ingredients in a mixing bowl.
3. Mist the waffle iron with cooking spray.
4. Drop half of the batter into the hot waffle iron and heat for 3-5 minutes. Do the same with the rest of the batter.
5. Mix the filling ingredients in a small bowl, make sure the mixture results smooth.
6. Split the filling mixture between two waffles and put in the refrigerator for 10 minutes.
7. Serve and enjoy!

NUTRITION

Calories 307, Protein 6.7g, Fat 7.2g, Cholesterol 93 mg, Carbohydrates 5g, Sugar 0.7g.

ROSEMARY PORK CHOPS CHAFFLE

INGREDIENTS

- 4 eggs
- 2 cups grated mozzarella cheese
- Pinch of nutmeg
- 2 tbsp sour cream
- 6 tbsp almond flour
- 2 tsp baking powder
- 2 tbsp olive oil
- pork chops
- 1 tsp freshly chopped rosemary
- 2 tbsp cooking spray
- 2 tbsp basil, freshly chopped
- Salt and pepper to taste

 SERVINGS: 4

 COOKING TIME: 15 MINUTES

HOW TO MAKE IT

1. Preheat the waffle maker.
2. Add the eggs, mozzarella cheese, salt and pepper, nutmeg, sour cream, almond flour and baking powder to a bowl. Mix until combined.
3. Brush the heated waffle maker with cooking spray and add a few tablespoons of the batter.
4. Close the lid and cook for about 7 minutes depending on your waffle maker.
5. Meanwhile, heat the butter in a nonstick grill pan and season the pork chops with salt and pepper and freshly chopped rosemary.
6. Cook the pork chops for about 4-5 minutes on each side.
7. Serve each chaffle with a pork chop and sprinkle some freshly chopped basil on top.

NUTRITION

Calories 366, fat 55.2 g, carbs 4.8 g, sugar 0.4 g, Protein 37.5 g, sodium 235 mg

PUMPKIN SPICE CHICKEN SAUSAGE CHAFFLE

INGREDIENTS

- 1/2 tsp. baking powder
- 1/2 cup cheddar cheese
- 1/4 cup egg whites
- 2 tsp. pumpkin spice
- 1 egg, whole
- 2 chicken sausage
- 2 slice bacon
- salt and pepper
- 1 tsp. avocado oil

 SERVINGS:3

 COOKING TIME: 10 MINUTES

HOW TO MAKE IT

1. Mix all ingredients.
2. Allow batter to sit while waffle iron warms.
3. Spray chaffle iron with nonstick spray.
4. Pour batter into the waffle maker and cook it.
5. Meanwhile, place the oil in a pan, when hot, fry the egg, according to your choice, and transfer it to a plate.
6. In the same pan, fry the bacon and sausage on medium heat for about 2-3 minutes until browned.
7. When chaffles are completely cooked , remove them from the maker.

NUTRITION

Protein: 22% 86 kcal Fat: 74% 286 kcal Carbohydrates: 3% 312 kcal

PARSLEY PORK CHAFFLES

INGREDIENTS

- ½ cup chopped parsley
- 1 cup pork
- 1 cup cheddar cheese
- 1 tbsp. avocado oil
- 1 egg
- A pinch of salt

SERVINGS: 4

COOKING TIME: 5 MINUTES

HOW TO MAKE IT

1. Warm your non-stick chaffle maker over medium heat.
2. Combine pork, parsley, cheese and egg in a bowl.
3. Coat the pan with avocado oil.
4. Once the pan is hot, add 2 tablespoons of pork paste and cook for about 1-2 minutes. Turn over and cook for another 1-2 minutes.
5. When the chaffles are brown, remove them from the pan.
6. Serve the BBQ sauce over it and enjoy!

NUTRITION

Carbohydrates: 2%, 345 kcal, Protein: 31%, Fat: 67%

MUSARD PORK CHAFFLE

INGREDIENTS

Filling:
- ½ tbsp Dijon mustard
- 25 g swiss cheese (sliced)
- 1 stalk celery (diced)
- 1 tsp paprika
- 3 slices pickle chips
- ½ tbsp mayonnaise
- 3 ounces pork roast
- 2 ounces cooked deli ham

Chaffle:
- 1 tbsp almond flour
- 1 tsp baking powder
- 4 tbsp mozzarella cheese
- 1 tbsp full-fat Greek yogurt
- 1 large egg (beaten)

SERVINGS: 1

COOKING TIME: 10 MINUTES

HOW TO MAKE IT

1. The oven must be preheated to 350°F and a baking sheet must be greased. Plug in the waffle iron to preheat it and spray it with non-stick cooking spray.
2. Combine the cheese, almond flour and baking powder in a bowl. Mix in the egg and yogurt. Blend until the ingredients are well combined.
3. Stuff the waffle iron with an adequate amount of the batter and expand it to the edges to cover all the wells of the waffle iron. Shut the waffle maker and cook the waffle until it is crunchy. This will take approximately 5 minutes. The time can be different on some waffle makers. When the cook cycle is complete, remove the waffle from the waffle iron with a plastic or silicone utensil.
4. Cook all of the batter in the waffles. Combine the mustard, oregano and mayonnaise in a small bowl.
5. Coat the surface of the two chamfers with the mustard-mayonnaise mixture. Arrange the pork, ham, pickles and celery on one of the waffles. Lay the cheese slices on top and cover with the second waffle. Put it on the baking sheet.
6. Place in the oven and bake until the cheese melts. You can set a heavy piece of stainless steel over the chaffle so that the sandwich will come out smooth and flat after baking.
7. Following the baking cycle, remove the chaffle sandwich from the oven and let it cool down. Serve hot and enjoy!

NUTRITION

Carbs 17.3g 6%, Fat 52.3g 67%, Protein 82.6g, Sugars 2.7g, 345 kcal

BARBEQUE SAUCE PORK CHAFFLE

INGREDIENTS

- ½ pound pork
- 3 eggs
- 1 cup mozzarella cheese, grated
- Salt and pepper to taste
- 1 teaspoon dried rosemary
- 1 clove garlic, minced
- 3 tablespoons sugar-free BBQ sauce
- 2 tablespoons butter to brush
- ¼ cup sugar-free BBQ sauce for serving
- ½ pound pork rinds for serving
- ¼ cup sugar-free BBQ sauce for serving

  SERVINGS:4

COOKING TIME:15 MINUTES

HOW TO MAKE IT

1. Preheat the waffle maker.
2. Add the ground pork, eggs, mozzarella, salt and pepper, minced garlic, dried rosemary, and BBQ sauce to a bowl.
3. Mix until all the ingredients are well combined. Brush the heated waffle maker with butter and add a few tablespoons of the batter.
4. Close the lid and cook for about 7– 8 minutes depending on your waffle maker.
5. Serve each chaffle with some pork rinds and a tablespoon of BBQ sauce.

NUTRITION

Calories 350, fat 21.1 g, carbs 2.g, sugar 0.3 g, Protein 36.9 g, sodium 801 mg

BEEF CHAFFLE

INGREDIENTS

- Batter
- ½ pound ground beef
- 4 eggs
- 4 ½ ounces cream cheese
- 1 cup grated mozzarella cheese
- Salt and pepper to taste
- ½ clove garlic, minced
- ½ tsp freshly chopped rosemary
- 2 tbsp butter to brush
- ¼ cup sour cream
- 2 tablespoons freshly chopped parsley for garnish

  SERVINGS:3

COOKING TIME: 10 MINUTES

HOW TO MAKE IT

1. Preheat the waffle maker.
2. Add the ground beef, eggs, cream cheese, grated mozzarella cheese, salt and pepper, minced garlic and freshly chopped rosemary to a bowl.
3. Brush the heated waffle maker with butter and add a few tablespoons of the batter.
4. Close the lid and cook for about 8–10 minutes depending on your waffle maker.
5. Serve each chaffle with a tablespoon of sour cream and freshly chopped parsley on top.

NUTRITION

Calories 368, fat 24 g, carbs 2.1 g, sugar 0.4 g, Protein 27.4 g, sodium 291 mg

GARLIC BEEF LIVER CHAFFLES

INGREDIENTS

- ½ cup shredded mozzarella cheese
- 1 tsp almond flour
- ¼ tsp garlic salt
- 1 egg
- 2 tbsp shredded parmesan cheese
- ½ tsp garlic powder
- 1/8 tsp Italian seasoning
- ¼ tsp baking powder
- 3 tsp unsalted butter (melted)
- 1 tbsp finely chopped cooked beef liver

Garnish:

- Chopped green onion

NUTRITION

Fat 18g 23%, Carbohydrate 4.5g 2%, Sugars 0.9g, Protein 12g, 315 kcal

 SERVINGS: 4

 COOKING TIME: 15 MINUTES

HOW TO MAKE IT

1. Heat the oven to 380°F and place a baking sheet with parchment paper.
2. Connect the waffle iron to preheat and spray with non-stick spray. Blend together the almond flour, Italian seasoning, baking powder, garlic powder, beef liver and cheese in a mixing bowl.
3. Next, add the egg and mix until well combined. Stuff the waffle maker with the appropriate amount of batter and distribute the batter to the edge of the waffle maker to cover all the holes in the waffle iron.
4. Shut the lid of the waffle iron and bake the waffles for about 4 minutes or according to the setting of the waffle iron. While this is happening, whisk together the garlic salt and melted butter in a bowl.
5. Remove the waffles from the waffle iron with a plastic or silicone tool when cooked.
6. Continue repeating steps 4, 5 and 7 until all the batter is baked into waffles and brush the surface of each waffle with the butter mixture. Spread Parmesan cheese over the chaffles and spread them on the lined baking tray.
7. Put the tray in the oven and bake for approximately 5 minutes or until the cheese has melted. Take the bread taffles out of the oven and leave them to cool for a few minutes.
8. Serve warm and garnish with chopped green onions.

CHICKEN CHAFFLE

INGREDIENTS

- ½ pound chicken
- 4 eggs
- 3 tablespoons tomato paste
- Salt and pepper to taste
- 1 cup grated mozzarella cheese
- 1 teaspoon dried oregano
- 2 tablespoons butter to brush the waffle maker

HOW TO MAKE IT

1. Preheat the waffle maker.
2. Add the ground chicken, eggs and tomato sauce to a bowl and season with salt and pepper.
3. Mix everything with a whisk, stir in the mozzarella cheese and oregano.
4. Mix again until everything is well combined. Brush the pre-heated waffle maker with butter and add a few tablespoons of the batter.
5. Close the lid and cook for about 8-10 minutes depending on your waffle maker.
6. Serve and enjoy.

 SERVINGS:4

 COOKING TIME: 10 MINUTES

NUTRITION

Calories 246, fat 15.6 g, carbs 1.5 g, sugar 0.9 g, Protein 24.2 g, sodium 254 mg

CHEDDAR, BROCCOLI & CHICKEN CHAFFLE

INGREDIENTS

- 1/4 cup cooked diced chicken
- 1/4 cup fresh broccoli chopped
- Shredded Cheddar cheese
- 1 egg
- 1/4 tsp garlic powder
- Pinch of Chili pepper

HOW TO MAKE IT

1. Heat up your waffle maker.
2. In a small bowl, mix the egg, garlic powder, and cheddar cheese. Add the broccoli and chicken and mix well.
3. Add 1/2 of the batter into your mini waffle maker and cook for 5 to 7 minutes. Cook then the rest of the batter to make a second chaffle and then make a third one.
4. After cooking, remove from the pan and let sit for 2 minutes.
5. Dip in ranch dressing, sour cream, or if you like it spicy add just a pinch of chili pepper. Enjoy!

 SERVINGS: 4

 COOKING TIME: 16 MINUTES

NUTRITION

Calories: 58kcal; Carbohydrates:1g; Protein: 19g; Fat: 3g;Saturated Fat:1g; Cholesterol:94mg ;Sodium:57mg ;Potassium: 136mg; Fiber: 1g ;Sugar: 1g ;Vitamin A: 190IU ;Vitamin C: 10mg ;Calcium: 18mg ;Iron: 1mg

ARTICHOKE AND SPINACH CHICKEN CHAFFLE

INGREDIENTS

- 1/3 cup cooked diced chicken
- 1/3 cup marinated artichokes, chopped
- 1/3 cup shredded mozzarella cheese
- 1/3 cup cooked spinach, chopped
- 1 ounce softened cream cheese
- 1/4 teaspoon garlic powder
- 1 egg

HOW TO MAKE IT

1. Heat up your waffle maker.
2. In a small bowl, mix the egg, garlic powder, cream cheese, and Mozzarella Cheese.
3. Add the spinach, the artichokes and the chicken. Mix well all the ingredients.
4. Add 1/3 of the batter into your waffle maker and cook your first chaffle for few minutes.
5. Repeat twice until you have three chaffle.
6. After cooking, remove from the pan and let them sit for 2 minutes.
7. Dip your chaffle in ranch dressing and sour cream.
8. Serve and enjoy!

SERVINGS: 2

COOKING TIME: 8 MINUTES

NUTRITION

Calories: 321kcal ;Carbohydrates:3g; Protein: 11g;Fat: 13g; Saturated Fat:6g ;Cholesterol:46mg ;Sodium:322mg ;Potassium: 140mg ; Fiber: 1g ;Sugar: 1g ;Vitamin A: 1119IU ;Vitamin C: 8mg ;Calcium: 115mg

- -

CHEESY PARMESAN CHICKEN CHAFFLES

INGREDIENTS

- 1 egg
- 1/3 cup chicken
- 1/3 cup mozzarella cheese
- 1/4 tsp basil
- 1/4 garlic
- 2 tbsp tomato sauce
- 2 tbsp Mozzarella cheese

HOW TO MAKE IT

1. Preheat your waffle maker. Preheat oven at 400 degrees.
2. Take a bowl, break your egg and beat it until the white and yolk look smooth.
3. And add the pre-cooked chicken, basil, garlic, and the mozzarella cheese previously greated.
4. Add 1/2 of the batter into your maker and cook for about 4 minutes.
5. Adjust the cooking time according to your waffle maker and your taste.
6. Then cook the rest of the batter.
7. When they look golden that's the time to remove them from the pan and let them sit for 2 minutes. Top your chaffle with 1-2 tablespoons sauce on each chicken parmesan chaffle.
8. Sprinkle 1-2 tablespoon mozzarella cheese for extra taste.
9. Place your chaffles in the oven and cook until the cheese is melted to add some crunchiness. Enjoy!

SERVINGS: 2

COOKING TIME: 8 MINUTES

NUTRITION

Calories: 285kcal; Carbohydrates:2g; Protein: 14g;Fat: 13g ; Cholesterol:122mg; Sodium:254mg; Potassium: 66mg ; Sugar: 1g

CREAMY TURKEY CHAFFLE SANDWICH

INGREDIENTS

- 4 eggs
- ¼ cup cream cheese
- 1 cup grated mozzarella cheese
- Salt and pepper to taste
- 1 teaspoon dried dill
- ½ teaspoon onion powder
- ½ teaspoon garlic powder
- 2 tablespoons butter
- 1 pound turkey breast
- 2 tablespoons heavy cream
- 2 tablespoons butter to brush
- 4 lettuce leaves to garnish
- 4 tomato slices to garnish

 SERVINGS: 4

 COOKING TIME: 15 MINUTES

HOW TO MAKE IT

1. Preheat the waffle maker.
2. Add the eggs, cream cheese, mozzarella cheese, salt and pepper, dried dill, onion powder and garlic powder to a bowl. Mix everything with a fork just until batter forms.
3. Brush the heated waffle maker with butter and add a few tablespoons of the batter.
4. Close the lid and cook for about 7 minutes depending on your waffle maker.
5. Meanwhile, heat some butter in a nonstick pan.
6. Season the turkey with salt and pepper and sprinkle with dried dill. Pour the heavy cream on top. Cook the chicken slices for about 10 minutes or until golden brown.
7. Cut each chaffle in half. On one half add a lettuce leaf, tomato slice, and chicken slice. Cover with the other chaffle half to make a sandwich.

NUTRITION

Calories 381, fat 26.3 g, carbs 2.5 g, sugar 1 g, Protein 32.9 g, sodium 278 mg

TASTY SAUSAGE GRAVY CHAFFLE

INGREDIENTS

- 1 egg
- 1 tsp coconut flour
- 1/4 tsp baking powder
- 1/2 cup mozzarella cheese
- Pinch of salt and pepper
- 1 tsp water
- 1/4 cup breakfast sausage
- 2 tsp cream cheese, softened
- Pepper to taste
- 3 tbsp chicken broth
- 2 tbsp heavy whipping cream
- Dash of onion powder (optional)
- Dash garlic powder

 SERVINGS: 2

 COOKING TIME: 10 MINUTES

HOW TO MAKE IT

1. Preheat the waffle maker and grease it lightly or diffuse some non-stick cooking spray.
2. Combine all the ingredients for the chaffles in a bowl, and mix thoroughly.
3. Transfer half of the batter to the maker, and let the chaffle cook for about 4 minutes.
4. Carefully take the chaffle out of the waffle iron and repeat to make a second one. Keep aside.
5. For the keto sausage gravy: Cook one pound of breakfast sausage and let strain. For this recipe we will need 1/4 cup.
6. Brown it and crumble it. Use the rest of the sausage to make sausage patties.
7. Wipe excess grease from pan and empty the 1/4 cup browned breakfast sausage and remaining ingredients.
8. Bring to a boil, while keep stirring it.
9. Lower the heat and continue to cook with the cover off, and make it thicken for about 5-7 minutes.
10. Let it cool off and it will settle more (if you want to add thickness you can add some xanthan gum).

NUTRITION

Calories: 322 kcal, Fiber: 1g,
Carbohydrates:3g, Saturated
Fat:10g, Potassium: 133mg,
Protein: 11g, Fat: 17g,
Cholesterol:134mg

II. Use salt and pepper to taste and gently spoon the gravy over the chaffles. Enjoy!

- -

JALAPENO CHICKEN CHAFFLE

INGREDIENTS

- ½ pound ground chicken
- 4 eggs
- 1 cup grated mozzarella cheese
- 2 tablespoons sour cream
- 1 green jalapeno, chopped
- Salt and pepper to taste
- 1 teaspoon dried oregano
- ½ teaspoon dried garlic
- 2 tablespoons butter to brush
- ¼ cup sour cream to garnish
- 1 green jalapeno, diced, to garnish

HOW TO MAKE IT

1. Preheat the waffle maker.
2. Add the ground chicken, eggs, mozzarella cheese, sour cream, chopped jalapeo, salt and pepper, dried oregano and dried garlic to a bowl.
3. Mix everything until batter forms. Brush the heated waffle maker with butter and add a few tablespoons of the batter.
4. Close the lid and cook for about 8-10 minutes depending on your waffle maker. Serve with a tablespoon of sour cream and sliced jalapeños on top.

SERVINGS: 4

COOKING TIME: 10 MINUTES

NUTRITION

Calories 284, fat 19.4 g, carbs 2.2 g, sugar 0.6 g, Protein 24.g, sodium 204 mg

TASTY LAMB BITES ON CHAFFLE

INGREDIENTS

- 4 medium eggs
- 2 cups grated mozzarella cheese
- ¼ cup heavy cream
- 1 teaspoon garlic powder
- 2 teaspoons baking powder
- 6 tablespoons almond flour
- 2 tablespoons butter to brush
- 2 tablespoons fresh parsley
- Salt and pepper to taste
- 2 tablespoons aromatic butter
- 1 pound lamb chops
- Salt and pepper to taste
- 1 teaspoon fresh rosemary

 SERVINGS:4

 COOKING TIME: 10 MINUTES

HOW TO MAKE IT

1. Heat the waffle maker.
2. Combine the eggs, mozzarella cheese, salt and pepper, garlic powder, heavy cream, almond flour and baking powder to a bowl.
3. Mix until the batter looks smooth.
4. Brush the heated waffle maker with butter and add a few tablespoons of the batter.
5. Close the lid and cook for about 7 minutes depending on your waffle maker.
6. Meanwhile, heat a nonstick frying pan and rub the lamb chops with aromatic butter, salt and pepper, and rosemary.
7. Cook the lamb for about 3-4 minutes on each side.
8. Serve each chaffle with a few lamb chops and sprinkle on some freshly chopped parsley for a nice presentation.

NUTRITION

Calories 246, fat 15.6 g, carbs 1.5 g, sugar 0.9 g, Protein 24.2 g, sodium 254 mg

TZATZIKI SAUCE PORK BITES CHAFFLE

INGREDIENTS

- 4 medium eggs
- 2 cups grated provolone cheese
- 1 teaspoon dried oregano
- 1 teaspoon dried rosemary
- Salt and pepper to taste
- 2 tablespoons butter to brush
- 1 pound pork tenderloin chopped
- 2 tablespoons olive oil
- Salt and pepper to taste
- 1 cup sour cream
- Salt and pepper as preferred
- 1 cucumber, peeled and diced
- 1 teaspoon dried dill
- 1 teaspoon garlic powder

 SERVINGS: 4

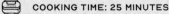 COOKING TIME: 25 MINUTES

HOW TO MAKE IT

1. Preheat the waffle maker.
2. Mix the eggs with your grated provolone cheese, rosemary, and dried oregano in a bowl.
3. Season the mixture with salt and pepper as you like.
4. Mix again until combined.
5. Brush the waffle maker with butter and add a few tablespoons of the batter you just made.
6. Close the lid and cook for 7 minutes. The timing may depend on your waffle maker.
7. Meanwhile, heat the olive oil in a nonstick frying pan. Season the pork tenderloin with salt and pepper and cook it for about 6 minutes, turn around and cook for another 5 to 6 minutes.
8. Mix the sour cream with diced cucumber, add salt and pepper, garlic powder and dried dill in another bowl.
9. Serve each chaffle with a few tablespoons of tzatziki sauce and bites of pork tenderloin.

NUTRITION

Calories 400, fat 50.g, carbs 6 g, sugar 1.5 g, Protein 54.4 g, sodium 777 mg

LAMB KEBAB ON CHAFFLE

INGREDIENTS

- 4 eggs
- 2 cups grated mozzarella cheese
- 1 tsp garlic powder
- Salt and pepper as desired
- ½ cup coconut flour
- ¼ cup Greek yogurt
- 2 tsp baking powder
- 2 tbsp butter to brush
- ¼ cup sour cream to serve
- 4 sprigs of fresh dill to garnish
- 1 pound lamb chops
- 2 tbsp almond flour
- 1 spring onion, finely chopped
- 1 egg
- 2 tbsp olive oil
- ½ tsp dried garlic

SERVINGS: 2

COOKING TIME: 8 MINUTES

HOW TO MAKE IT

1. Preheat the waffle maker.
2. Mix together the eggs, the mozzarella cheese, salt and pepper, garlic powder, greek yogurt, coconut flour and baking powder in a large bowl.
3. Brush the heated waffle maker with butter and add a few tablespoons of the batter.
4. Close the lid and cook for about 7 minutes depending on your waffle maker.
5. Meanwhile, add the ground lamb, salt and pepper, egg, almond flour, chopped spring onion, and dried garlic to a bowl.
6. Mix and form medium-sized kebabs.
7. Impale each kebab on a skewer. Heat the olive oil in a frying pan. Cook the lamb kebabs for about 3 minutes on each side.
8. Serve each chaffle with a tablespoon of sour cream and one or two lamb kebabs.
9. Decorate with fresh dill.

NUTRITION

Calories 479, fat 49.9 g, carbs 15.8 g, sugar 0.8 g, Protein 42.6 g, sodium 302 mg

CHAFFLE BEEFSTEAK

INGREDIENTS

- 1 beefsteak rib eye
- 1 tsp salt
- 1 tsp pepper
- 1 tbsp. lime juice
- 1 tsp garlic
- 2 whole eggs
- 4 oz. cheese
- 2 oz. almond flour
- 1/4 cup almond flour
- 1 tsp baking powder

SERVINGS: 2

COOKING TIME: 8 MINUTES

HOW TO MAKE IT

1. Prepare your grill for direct heat.
2. Mix all ingredients for the chaffle and cook for around 5 minutes in your pre-heated maker.
3. Mix all spices and rub over the beefsteak equally.
4. Place the beef on the grill rack over medium heat.
5. Cover and cook steak for about 6 to 8 minutes.
6. Flip and cook for another 5 minutes until cooked.
7. Cut it in small slices and lay them over your chaffle.
8. Sprinkle few drops of lime.

NUTRITION

Protein: 51% 274 kcal Fat: 45% 343 kcal Carbohydrates: 4% 22 kcal

CHICKEN CHEDDAR CHAFFLE

INGREDIENTS

- ¼ tsp taco seasoning
- 1 egg, beaten
- 1/3 cup cooked chicken
- 1/3 cup finely grated cheddar cheese

SERVINGS: 2

COOKING TIME: 14 MINUTES

HOW TO MAKE IT

1. Preheat the waffle iron. Combine eggs, taco seasoning and cheddar cheese in a medium bowl.
2. Mix in the chicken and combine well. Flip the griddle open, lightly grease with cooking spray and pour in half of the mixture.
3. Cook until browny and crispy, for about 7 minutes.
4. Retire the chaffle to a plate and set aside. Do another chaffle with the remaining mixture.
5. Serve later and enjoy!

NUTRITION

Calories 314, Fats 20.64g, Carbs 5.71g, Net Carbs 5.71g, Protein 16.74g

CHEESY BACON SALAD CHAFFLE

INGREDIENTS

- 4 eggs
- 1½ cups grated mozzarella
- 1 tsp dried oregano
- ½ cup parmesan cheese
- ¼ cup almond flour
- Salt and pepper to taste
- 2 tbsp baking powder
- For the Bacon salad:
- ½ pound cooked bacon
- 1 cup cream cheese
- 1 tsp dried basil
- 1 tsp dried oregano
- 1 tsp dried rosemary
- 2 tablespoons lemon juice
- Other:
- 2 spring onions, finely chopped, for serving
- 2 tbsp butter to brush the waffle maker

SERVINGS: 1

COOKING TIME: 15 MINUTES

HOW TO MAKE IT

1. Preheat the waffle maker.
2. Add the eggs, mozzarella cheese, parmesan cheese, salt and pepper, dried oregano, almond flour and baking powder to a bowl.
3. Mix until combined.
4. Brush the heated waffle maker with butter and add a few tablespoons of the batter.
5. Close the lid and cook for about 7 minutes depending on your waffle maker.
6. Meanwhile, chop the cooked bacon into smaller pieces and place them in a bowl with the cream cheese. Season with dried oregano, dried basil, dried rosemary and lemon juice.
7. Mix until combined and spread each chaffle with the creamy bacon salad.
8. To serve, sprinkle some freshly chopped spring onion on top.

NUTRITION

Calories 750, fat 62.5 g, carbs 7.7 g, sugar 0.8 g, Protein 40.3 g, sodium 1785 mg

CHEESEBURGER CHAFFLE

INGREDIENTS

- For the Cheeseburgers:
- 1/3 pound ground beef
- 2 slices American cheese
- ½ tsp garlic salt
- For the sauce:
- 1 tsp mayonnaise
- 1 tsp dill pickle relish
- ½ tsp ketchup
- splash of vinegar, to taste
- For the Chaffles:
- 1 large egg
- 1/2 cup mozzarella, shredded
- 1/4 tsp garlic salt

NUTRITION

Calories: 831 Total Fat: 56g, Saturated Fat: 23g, Trans Fat: 2g, Unsaturated Fat: 26g, Sodium: 3494mg Carbohydrates: 8g, Sugar: 2g, Protein: 4

 SERVINGS: 1

 COOKING TIME: 15 MINUTES

HOW TO MAKE IT

1. For the chaffles:
2. Heat the mini waffle maker and spray the non-stick spray.
3. Mix the egg, cheese, and garlic salt.
4. Add half of the egg mixture to the waffle iron and cook for 2-3 minutes.
5. Set aside and repeat with the rest of the batter.
6. To prepare the burgers: Heat a griddle over medium-high heat.
7. Distant 6 inches from each other, place 2 equal sized balls of ground beef.
8. As you start to cook them, press them firmly straight down until flatten (use a small salad plate or something else sturdy and flat).
9. Drizzle with garlic salt.
10. After 2 minutes flip the burgers delicately and spatter with remaining garlic salt. Finish cooking other 2 minutes or until cooked as preferred.
11. Lay one slice of cheese over each patty, stack them and set them aside on a plate. Cover with foil.
12. To make the sauce, put together all ingredients and whisk.
13. Place the stacked burger patties on one chaffle, and above it the shredded lettuce, onions, and pickles.
14. Spread the sauce on the other chaffle and place and close the burger with it.
15. Eat immediately and enjoy!

ITALIAN TINY MEATBALLS CHAFFLE

INGREDIENTS

- 4 eggs
- 2½ cups grated gouda cheese
- 1 spring onion, chopped
- ¼ cup heavy cream
- Salt and pepper to taste
- 1 pound ground beef
- Salt and pepper as desired
- 1 spring onion, finely chopped
- 2 teaspoons Dijon mustard
- 2 tablespoons butter
- 5 tablespoons almond flour
- 2 tablespoons fresh parsley
- 2 tablespoons cooking spray

 SERVINGS: 4

 COOKING TIME: 20 MINUTES

HOW TO MAKE IT

1. Preheat the waffle maker.
2. Add the eggs, grated gouda cheese, heavy cream, salt and pepper and finely chopped spring onion to a bowl.
3. Whisk until combined.
4. Brush the heated waffle maker with cooking spray and add a few tablespoons of the batter.
5. Close the lid and cook for about 7 minutes depending on your waffle maker.
6. Meanwhile, mix the ground beef meat, salt and pepper, Dijon mustard, chopped spring onion and almond flour in a large bowl.

NUTRITION

Calories 670, fat 47.4g, carbs 4.6 g, sugar 1.7 g, Protein 54.9 g, sodium 622 mg

- -

CHEDDAR, BROCCOLI & CHICKEN CHAFFLE

INGREDIENTS

- 1 tsp paprika
- 1 stalk celery (diced)
- 3 slices pickle chips
- 25 g swiss cheese (sliced)
- 2 ounces cooked deli ham
- ½ tbsp Dijon mustard
- ½ tbsp mayonnaise
- 3 ounces pork roast
- 1 tbsp almond flour
- 1 tbsp full-fat Greek yogurt
- 1 tsp baking powder
- 4 tbsp mozzarella cheese
- 1 large egg (beaten)

HOW TO MAKE IT

1. Heat the oven to 350°F and grease a baking tray.
2. Connect the waffle iron to preheat it and spray it with non-stick cooking spray. Blend the almond flour, cheese and baking powder in a mixing bowl.
3. Next, add the egg and yoghurt.
4. Mix until the ingredients are well combined. Add an appropriate amount of batter to the waffle iron and distribute the batter to the edges so that all the holes in the waffle iron are coated.
5. Shut the waffle iron and bake the waffle until it is crispy. This will take about 4 minutes.
6. Time may vary on some waffle irons.
7. Remove the waffle from the waffle iron after cooking using a plastic or silicone utensil.
8. Continue repeating steps 4 to 6 until you have baked all the batter into waffles.
9. Combine the mustard, oregano and mayonnaise in a small bowl. Coat the mustard-mayonnaise mixture over the surface of the two chaffles.
10. Put the pork, ham, pickles and celery on one of the skewers.

NUTRITION

Fat 52.3g 67%, Carbs 17.3g 6%,
Sugars 2.7g, Protein 82.6g,
Calories 370

 SERVINGS: 4

 COOKING TIME: 16 MINUTES

11. Arrange the cheese slices on top and cover with the second spindle. Put it on the baking tray. Put it in the oven and bake until the cheese melts. You may place a heavy, stainless steel base over the chaffle to help the sandwich flatten after baking. Remove the Chaffle sandwich from the oven when baked and leave to cool down for a 5 minutes.

12. Then serve warm and enjoy.

CHEESY CHICKEN CHAFFLE

INGREDIENTS

- ½ tsp dried basil
- 2 ounces cream cheese
- 2 tbsp buffalo sauce
- ½ tsp garlic powder
- 5 ounces cooked chicken (diced)
- ½ tsp onion powder
- 1 egg
- 5 tbsp shredded cheddar cheese

NUTRITION

Fat 20.1g 26%, Carbohydrate 2.2g
1%, Sugars 0.7g, Protein 30g,
Calories 570

 SERVINGS: 2

 COOKING TIME: 10 MINUTES

HOW TO MAKE IT

1. Plug in the waffle iron and preheat it.
2. Apply non-stick spray to the waffle iron. Together in a mixing bowl, combine the onion powder, basil, garlic, buffalo sauce, cheddar cheese and cream cheese.
3. Stir the ingredients until they are well mixed and a smooth batter has formed.
4. Spread some grated cheddar cheese over the waffle iron and pour in an good amount of the batter.
5. Distribute the batter to the edges of the waffle iron so that all the holes in the waffle iron are covered.
6. Shut the lid of the waffle iron and bake the waffles for approximately 3 to minutes or according to the setting of the waffle iron.
7. When done, remove the waffles from the waffle iron using a plastic or silicone tool.
8. Continue repeating steps 3 to 5 until you have baked all the batter into waffles.
9. Serve and enjoy!

CHEESY BROCCOLI CHAFFLE

INGREDIENTS

- 4 eggs
- 1 cup steamed broccoli,
- 2 cups grated mozzarella cheese
- Salt and pepper to taste
- 1 teaspoon chili flakes
- 1 clove garlic, minced
- 2 teaspoons baking powder
- 2 tablespoons almond flour
- ¼ cup mascarpone cheese
- 2 tablespoons cooking spray

HOW TO MAKE IT

I. Preheat the waffle maker.

2. In a mixing bowl, combine the eggs, shredded mozzarella cheese, minced broccoli, salt and pepper, finely chopped garlic, chilli flakes, almond flour and baking powder.

3. Toss with a large fork.

4. Brush the heated waffle iron with cooking spray and add a couple of tablespoons of batter. Close the lid and cook for about 7 minutes according to your waffle maker.

5. Arrange each waffle with mascarpone cheese on top. Serve and enjoy!

SERVINGS:4

COOKING TIME:15 MINUTES

NUTRITION

Calories 329, fat 15 g, carbs 6 g, sugar 1.1 g, Protein 13.1 g, sodium 194 mg

---

CELERY AND COTTAGE CHEESE CHAFFLE

INGREDIENTS

- 4 eggs
- 2 cups grated cheddar cheese
- 1 cup fresh celery, chopped
- Salt and pepper to taste
- 2 tablespoons chopped almonds
- 2 teaspoons baking powder
- 2 tablespoons cooking spray to brush the waffle maker
- ¼ cup cottage cheese for serving

HOW TO MAKE IT

I. Preheat the waffle maker. Add the eggs, grated mozzarella cheese, chopped celery, salt and pepper, chopped almonds and baking powder to a bowl.

2. Mix with a fork.

3. Brush the heated waffle maker with cooking spray and add a few tablespoons of the batter.

4. Close the lid and cook for about 7 minutes depending on your waffle maker. Serve each chaffle with cottage cheese on top.

SERVINGS: 4

COOKING TIME: 15 MINUTES

NUTRITION

Calories 385, fat 31.6 g, carbs 4 g, sugar 1.5 g, Protein 22.2 g, sodium 492 mg

ZUCCHINI & ONION CHAFFLES

INGREDIENTS

- 2 cups zucchini, grated and squeezed
- ½ cup onion, grated and squeezed
- 2 organic eggs
- ½ cup Mozzarella cheese, shredded
- ½ cup Parmesan cheese, grated

HOW TO MAKE IT

1. Preheat you waffle maker and grease it.
2. In a medium bowl, place all ingredients and, mix until well combined.
3. Place ¼ of the mixture into preheated waffle iron and cook for about 4 minutes or until golden brown. Repeat with the remaining mixture. Serve warm.

SERVINGS: 4

COOKING TIME: 16 MINUTES

NUTRITION

Calories: 392 Net Carb: 2.Fat: 5.3g Saturated Fat: 2.3g Carbohydrates: 3.5g Dietary Fiber: 0.9g Sugar: 1.8g Protein: 8.6g

---

ZUCCHINI CHAFFLES

INGREDIENTS

- 2 large zucchinis, grated and squeezed
- 2 large organic eggs
- 2/3 cup Cheddar cheese, shredded
- 2 tablespoons coconut flour
- ½ teaspoon garlic powder
- ½ teaspoon red pepper flakes, crushed
- Salt, to taste

HOW TO MAKE IT

1. Preheat a waffle iron and then grease it.
2. In a medium bowl, place all ingredients and, mix until well combined.
3. Place ¼ of the mixture into preheated waffle iron and cook for about 4-4½ minutes or until golden brown. Repeat with the remaining mixture. Serve warm.

SERVINGS: 4

COOKING TIME: 18 MINUTES

NUTRITION

Calories: 159 Net Carb: 4.3g Fat: 10g Saturated Fat: 5.8g Carbohydrates: 8g Dietary Fiber: 3.7g Sugar: 2.Protein: 10.1g, Calories 370

BROCCOLI & ALMOND FLOUR CHAFFLES

INGREDIENTS

- 1 tablespoon almond flour
- 1 organic egg, beaten
- ¼ cup fresh broccoli, chopped
- ½ cup Cheddar cheese, shredded
- ¼ teaspoon garlic powder

HOW TO MAKE IT

1. Preheat a mini waffle iron and oil it.
2. Into a bowl, place all the ingredients and mix until well combined.
3. Put half of the mixture in the pre-heated chaffle iron and cook for about 4 minutes or until golden brown.
4. Do the same with the rest of the mixture.
5. Serve hot and enjoy!

 SERVINGS: 2

 COOKING TIME: 8 MINUTES

NUTRITION

Calories: 373, Net Carb: 1.5g, Fat: 13.5g, Saturated Fat: 8g, Carbohydrates: 2.2g, Dietary Fiber: 0.7g, Sugar: 0.7g, Protein: 10.2g

MOZZARELLA AND ASPARAGUS CHAFFLE

INGREDIENTS

- ¼ cup almond flour
- 2 teaspoons baking powder
- 1 cup boiled asparagus, chopped
- 1½ cups grated mozzarella cheese
- ½ cup grated parmesan cheese
- ¼ cup chopped almonds
- Salt and pepper to taste
- 4 eggs
- ¼ cup Greek yogurt for serving
- Other 2 tablespoons cooking spray to brush the waffle maker

HOW TO MAKE IT

1. Warm up the waffle iron. In a bowl, add the eggs, grated mozzarella, grated Parmesan, asparagus, salt and pepper, almond flour and baking powder.
2. Grease the heated waffle iron with cooking spray and put a few tablespoons of the batter in.
3. Shut the lid and let the waffles cook for approximately 7 minutes, according to the waffle iron.
4. Top each waffle with Greek yoghurt and chopped almonds.

 SERVINGS: 4

COOKING TIME: 15 MINUTES

NUTRITION

Calories 316, fat 24.9 g, carbs 3 g, sugar 1.2 g, Protein 18.2 g, sodium 261 mg.

MUSHROOM AND ALMOND CHAFFLE

INGREDIENTS

- 4 eggs
- 2 cups grated mozzarella cheese
- 1 cup finely chopped zucchini
- 3 tablespoons chopped almonds
- 2 teaspoons baking powder
- Salt and pepper to taste
- 1 teaspoon dried basil
- 1 teaspoon chili flakes
- 2 tablespoons cooking spray to brush the waffle maker

HOW TO MAKE IT

1. Preheat the waffle maker.
2. Add the eggs, grated mozzarella, mushrooms, almonds, baking powder, salt and pepper, dried basil and chili flakes to a bowl.
3. Mix with a fork.
4. Brush the heated waffle maker with cooking spray and add a few tablespoons of the batter.
5. Close the lid and cook for about 7 minutes depending on your waffle maker. Serve and enjoy.

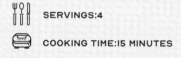 SERVINGS:4

COOKING TIME:15 MINUTES

NUTRITION

Calories 196, fat 16 g, carbs 4 g, sugar 1 g, Protein 10.8 g, sodium 152 mg

. . . .

HEALTHY BROCCOLI CHAFFLES

INGREDIENTS

- 1 pinch garlic powder
- A pinch salt
- 1 egg
- 1 tbsp. coconut oil
- ½ cup broccoli chopped
- 1 cup cheddar cheese
- 1 pinch black pepper
- 1 tsp baking powder

HOW TO MAKE IT

1. Warm your non-stick pan over a medium heat.
2. Mix all the ingredients together in a bowl. Brush the pan with oil.
3. When the pan is hot, place the broccoli and cheese paste in the greased pan and let cook for 1-2 minutes.
4. Cook for another 1-2 minutes, flipping the chaffles.
5. Remove from the pan as soon as the chaffles are brown.
6. Garnish with raspberries and melted coconut oil.
7. Enjoy your meal!

 SERVINGS: 4

 COOKING TIME: 5 MINUTES

NUTRITION

Protein: 20% Fat: 72%, Carbohydrates: 7% 315 kcal.

OKONOMIYAKI CHAFFLE

INGREDIENTS

- 1 tbsp green onion, chopped
- 1 tsp tamari sauce
- 2 eggs
- 1/3 cup mozzarella cheese, shredded
- 1 slice of bacon (finely chopped)
- A pinch of salt
- 4 tbsp finely shredded cabbage
- 1/8 tsp ground black pepper
- 2 tsp Worcestershire sauce
- 2 tbsp bonito flakes
- 1 tbsp kewpie mayonnaise or American mayonnaise

 SERVINGS: 1

 COOKING TIME: 10 MINUTES

HOW TO MAKE IT

1. Preheat a frying pan on medium-high heat and then add the chopped bacon. Fry until the bacon is brown and crispy.
2. Use a spoon to remove the bacon to a plate lined with paper towels to drain.
3. Connect the waffle iron to preheat and spray with non-stick spray.
4. Combine the crispy bacon, cabbage, cheese, onion, pepper and salt in a mixing bowl. Include the egg and tamari.
5. Blend until the ingredients are well combined. Then pour an adequate amount of batter into the waffle iron and distribute the batter so that all the holes in the waffle iron are covered.
6. Shut the waffle iron and cook the waffles for about 4 minutes or depending on the settings of your waffle iron.
7. Use a silicone or plastic utensil to remove the waffles from the waffle iron after cooking.
8. Continue repeating steps 5 to 7 until you have cooked all the batter into waffles. Spread sauce, mayonnaise and bonito flakes on top of the chaffles.
9. Serve warm and enjoy!

NUTRITION

Fat 23.3g 30%, Carbohydrate 9.1g 3%, Sugars 4.3g, Protein 22.9g, Calories 370

GARLIC CAULIFLOWER RICE CHAFFLE

INGREDIENTS

- 1 green onion (chopped)
- 4 tbsp shredded cheddar cheese
- ¼ tsp onion powder
- 1 egg
- ½ cup cauliflower rice
- ¼ tsp salt
- ½ tsp garlic powder

NUTRITION

Fat 6.9g 9%, Carbohydrate 2.9g 1%, Sugars 1.2g, Protein 7.1g, Calories 270

HOW TO MAKE IT

1. Place the cauliflower rice in a microwave-safe bowl and then cover the bowl. Put the bowl in the microwave and heat for 3 minutes. Take the bowl out of the microwave and stir.
2. Set it back in the microwave and stew it for about 1 minute or until soft. Let the cauliflower cool down for a few minutes.
3. Cover the steamed cauliflower in a clean towel and press it out to remove any excess water. Connect the waffle iron to preheat and spray with non-stick cooking spray.
4. Combine the cauliflower, green onion, onion powder, cheese, salt and garlic in a mixing bowl. Include the egg and mix the ingredients until well combined.
5. Put an appropriate amount of the batter into your waffle maker and spread the batter so that all the holes of the waffle iron are covered. Shut the waffle iron and bake until the waffles are golden brown.

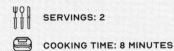

SERVINGS: 2

COOKING TIME: 8 MINUTES

6. Depending on the waffle iron, this will take about 4 minutes or lon-ger. Use a plastic or silicone utensil to remove the waffles from the waffle iron after cooking. Do steps 4 again until you have baked all the batter into waffles. Serve the Hash Brown Chaffles and top with your desired toppings.

SPINACH AND ARTICHOKE CHAFFLE

INGREDIENTS

- 4 eggs
- 2 cups grated provolone cheese
- 1 cup cooked and diced spinach
- ½ cup diced artichoke hearts
- Salt and pepper to taste
- 2 tablespoons coconut flour
- 2 teaspoons baking powder
- 2 tablespoons cooking spray to brush the waffle maker
- ¼ cup of cream cheese for serving

NUTRITION

Calories 342 fat 32.8 g, carbs 9.5 g, sugar 1.1 g, Protein 25.7 g

HOW TO MAKE IT

1. Preheat the waffle maker.
2. Add the eggs, grated provolone cheese, diced spinach, artichoke hearts, salt and pepper, coconut flour and baking powder to a bowl. Mix with a fork.
3. Brush the heated waffle maker with cooking spray and add a few tablespoons of the batter.
4. Close the lid and cook for about 7 minutes depending on your waf-fle maker.
5. Serve each chaffle with cream cheese.

SERVINGS: 2

COOKING TIME: 15 MINUTES

AROMATIC ZUCCHINI CHAFFLE

INGREDIENTS

- 1 teaspoon dried basil
- ¼ cup mozzarella cheese, shredded
- Pinch of aalt and pepper to taste
- 1 egg, beaten
- 1 cup zucchini, grated
- ½ cup Parmesan cheese, shredded
- Italian herbs

SERVINGS: 2

COOKING TIME: 8 MINUTES

HOW TO MAKE IT

1. Warm up your waffle iron. Drizzle a pinch of salt over the zucchini and mix. Leave to rest for 2 minutes.
2. Roll the zucchini in a paper towel and squeeze to remove the water.
3. Place in a bowl and add the rest of the ingredients.
4. Add half of the mixture into the waffle iron.
5. Seal the appliance and cook for 4 minutes. Prepare the second waffle following the same steps.
6. Serve and enjoy!

NUTRITION

Calories 294 Dietary Fiber 1 g Total Fat 13 g Total Carbohydrate 4 g Satura-ted Fat 7 g Sodium 789 mg Cholesterol 115 mg   Potassium 223 mg   Protein 16 g Total Sugars 2 g

79

TASTY SPINACH AND RICOTTA CHAFFLES

INGREDIENTS

- 2 eggs, beaten
- ½ cup finely grated mozzarella cheese
- 4 oz frozen spinach, thawed, squeezed dry
- ½ tsp. garlic powder
- 1 cup ricotta cheese
- ground black pepper to taste
- ¼ cup finely grated Pecorino Romano cheese
- Pinch of salt

HOW TO MAKE IT

1. Heat the waffle iron. Mix all the ingredients in a medium bowl. Open the griddle, lightly spray with cooking spray and pour in one-fourth of the mixture. Shut the iron and cook until golden brown and crisp, 7 minutes. Move the chaffle to a plate and set aside. Prepare three more chaffles with the remaining mixture. Leave to cool and serve later.
2. Serve and enjoy!

  SERVINGS: 4

COOKING TIME: 28 MINUTES

NUTRITION

Calories 300, Carbs 5.06g, Fats 13.15g, Protein 12.79g, Net Carbs 4.06g.

- -

HEALTHY ZUCCHINI CHAFFLES

INGREDIENTS

- 1 egg
- 1 cup zucchini, grated
- 1 tbsp. avocado oil
- A pinch of salt
- 1 cup cheddar cheese

HOW TO MAKE IT

1. Warm your non-stick pan at a medium heat. Salt the grated courgettes and leave them for 5 minutes.
2. In a small bowl, mix the courgettes, egg and cheese together.
3. Grease pan with avocado oil.
4. When the pan is hot, add 2 tablespoons of courgette batter and fry for around 1-2 minutes.
5. Turn and fry for another 1-2 minutes. When the chaffle is brown, remove from the pan.
6. Garnish with coconut cream and enjoy!

  SERVINGS: 4

COOKING TIME: 5 MINUTES

NUTRITION

Fat: 77%, Protein: 21%, Carbohydrates: 2%, 200 kcal.

PSYLLIUM HUSK CHAFFLE

INGREDIENTS

- 1 large organic egg, beaten
- ½ cup Mozzarella cheese, shredded
- ¼ teaspoon organic baking powder
- ½ teaspoon Psyllium husk powder
- 2 tablespoons blanched almond flour

HOW TO MAKE IT

1. Preheat a mini waffle iron and grease it.
2. Put all ingredients in a bowl and stir until well mixed.
3. Put half of the mixture in the preheated waffle iron and cook for about 4 minutes or until golden brown.
4. Continue with the rest of the mixture. Serve hot and enjoy!

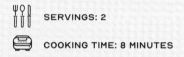
SERVINGS: 2

COOKING TIME: 8 MINUTES

NUTRITION

Calories: 301, Net Carb: 1g, Fat: 7.1g, Saturated Fat: 1.8g, Carbohydrates: 2.9.

CARROT AND WALNUTS CHAFFLES

INGREDIENTS

- 2 teaspoons cinnamon
- 1 egg, beaten
- 1 teaspoon baking powder
- 2 tablespoons heavy whipping cream
- 1 tablespoon walnuts, chopped
- ½ cup carrot, shredded
- 2 tablespoons melted butter
- ¾ cup almond flour
- 2 tablespoons sweetener
- 1 teaspoon pumpkin spice

HOW TO MAKE IT

1. Preheat your waffle iron. In a bowl, combine the ingredients.
2. Place some of the mixture into the waffle iron.
3. Seal and cook for a few minutes.
4. Continue repeating the steps until all of the remaining batter has been used.

SERVINGS: 6

COOKING TIME: 24 MINUTES

NUTRITION

Calories 294, Total Fat 27g, Saturated Fat 12g, Potassium 421mg, Cholesterol 133mg, Total Carbohydrate 11.6g, Sodium 144 mg, , Dietary Fiber 4.5g, Protein 6.8g, Total Sugars 1.7g

PECORINO ROMANO AND SPINACH CHAFFLES

INGREDIENTS

- ½ cup finely grated mozzarella cheese
- 1 cup ricotta cheese
- ¼ cup finely grated Pecorino Romano cheese
- ½ tsp garlic powder
- 4 oz frozen spinach, thawed, squeezed dry
- 2 eggs, beaten
- Salt to taste
- ground black pepper to taste

 SERVINGS: 4

 COOKING TIME: 28 MINUTES

HOW TO MAKE IT

1. Heat the waffle iron. In a medium bowl, mix all the ingredients. Open the iron, lightly grease with cooking spray and add a quarter of the mixture.
2. Shut the iron and cook until golden brown and crisp, 7 minutes.
3. Transfer the chaffle to a plate and set aside.
4. Use remaining chaffle mixture to make three more chaffles.
5. Let cool and serve later

NUTRITION

Calories 300, Fats 13.15g, Carbs 5.06g, Net Carbs 4.06g, Protein 12.79g

PUMPKIN SPICE THANKSGIVING CHAFFLE

CHRISTMAS MORNING COOKIE CHAFFLE

INGREDIENTS

- 4 ground eggs
- 1 tsp vanilla extract
- ¼ cup heavy cream
- 6 tbsp coconut flour
- 1 tsp baking powder
- ¼ cup stevia
- Pinch of salt
- ¼ cup unsweetened chocolate chips
- cooking spray to grease the waffle iron
- ¼ cup heavy cream, whipped

 SERVINGS:4

 COOKING TIME:7—9 MINUTES

HOW TO MAKE IT

1. Preheat the waffle maker.
2. Place in a medium bowl the eggs and the heavy cream.
3. Stir in with the vanilla extract, stevia, coconut flour, baking powder, and salt. Whisk well until the batter results smooth.
4. Combine the chocolate chips and stir again. Brush the preheated waffle maker with cooking spray and add half of the mixture.
5. Cook for about 7–8 minutes depending on your waffle maker.
6. Repeat with the remaining mixture. Serve with whipped cream on top.

NUTRITION

Calories 360, fat 32.3 g, carbs 12.6 g, sugar 0.5 g, Protein 9 g

. . . .

PUMPKIN SPICE THANKSGIVING CHAFFLE

INGREDIENTS

- 1 cup egg whites
- 2 tsps pumpkin pie spice
- 1 cup mozzarella cheese, grated
- ¼ cup pumpkin puree
- ½ tsp vanilla
- 2 tsps coconut flour
- 1 tsp. baking soda
- 1 tsp. baking powder
- 1/8 tsp cinnamon powder
- 1/2 tsp garlic powder

 SERVINGS: 4

 COOKING TIME: 5MINUTES

HOW TO MAKE IT

1. Preheat a mini waffle maker and spray it with a non-stick spray to make sure the surface is greased.
2. Beat egg whites, until you have a soft mixture.Place the pumpkin puree, pumpkin pie spice and the coconut flour in egg mixture. Whisk again.
3. Add the cheese, cinnamon powder, garlic powder, baking soda, and powder. Stir.
4. Pour ½ of the batter in the waffle maker and cook for about 3 minutes.
5. Repeat with the rest of the mixture.
6. Remove chaffles from the maker. Serve warm!
7. Tip: For extra flavour you may want to serve with a scoop of whipped cream and some cinnamon powder on top.

NUTRITION

Protein: 51% 660 kcal Fat: 41% Carbohydrates: 8%

FALL SPICY PUMPKIN CHAFFLES

INGREDIENTS

- 1 ground egg
- ½ tsp pumpkin pie spice
- 1 tbsp pumpkin puree
- ½ cup mozzarella cheese, grated
- 1/4 cup walnuts, chopped

HOW TO MAKE IT

1. Turn your waffle maker on and as it gets warm spray it with a non-stick spray.
2. Take a bowl, stir all the ingredients together until smooth.
3. Place half of the batter in the waffle maker, close, and cook for 6 minutes, or until golden.
4. Repeat the process with the remaining mixture. Drizzle chopped walnuts on them. Enjoy!

SERVINGS: 2

COOKING TIME: 14 MINUTES

NUTRITION

Calories 395, Fats 6.46g, Carbs 1.98g, Net Carbs 1.58g, Protein 5.94g

INDEPENDENCE DAY CHAFFLE SNACKS

INGREDIENTS

- 1 ground egg
- ½ cup finely grated cheddar cheese
- Raspberries and blueberries for topping
- ½ cup Greek yogurt

HOW TO MAKE IT

1. Preheat a waffle maker and grease it.
2. Beat the egg and cheddar cheese together in a bowl.
3. Place half of the batter in the waffle maker, close, and cook for 6 to 7 minutes.
4. Repeat the prices with the remaining mixture.
5. Cut the chaffle into wedges and top each of them with a tablespoon of greek yogurt. Add two berries.
6. Serve and enjoy with friends and family!

SERVINGS: 2

COOKING TIME: 14 MINUTES

NUTRITION

Calories 307, Fats 15.29g, Carbs 4.36g, Net Carbs 3.g, Protein 12.91g

RASPBERRIES AND PEANUT BUTTER CHAFFLE

INGREDIENTS

- 1 ground egg
- ½ cup cheddar cheese, grated finely
- 2 cups peanut butter
- 16 oz. raspberries

 SERVINGS:8

 COOKING TIME:5MINUTES

HOW TO MAKE IT

1. Preheat a waffle maker and spray it with a non-stick spray.
2. Take a bowl, stir all the cheese and the egg together until smooth.
3. Place half of the batter in the waffle maker, close, and cook for 6 to 7 minutes.
4. Repeat the prices with the remaining mixture. Allow cooling.
5. Assemble your chaffles in layers. Coat each layer with peanut butter and top with raspberries.
6. Enjoy on Christmas morning with your family!

NUTRITION

Protein: 3% Fat: 94% Carbohydrates: 3%, 350 Kcal

....

CARROT AND WALNUTS CHAFFLES

INGREDIENTS

- Pizza Filing:
- ½ cup shredded mozzarella cheese
- 1 small green bell pepper (finely chopped)
- 1 tbsp marinara sauce
- 1 onion (finely chopped)
- 1/3 cups pepperoni slices
- Chaffle:
- A pinch of Italian seasoning
- 1 beaten egg
- ½ tsp dried basil leaves
- 1 tbsp almond flour
- A pinch of salt
- ¼ tsp baking powder

 SERVINGS: 2

 COOKING TIME: 15 MINUTES

HOW TO MAKE IT

1. Pre-heat oven to 400°F and cover a baking sheet with parchment paper. Turn on the waffle iron and preheat it.
2. Mist with non-stick spray.
3. For the waffle: In a bowl, combine garlic powder, baking powder, Italian seasoning, almond flour, basil, mozzarella and salt.
4. Stir in the egg and blend until the ingredients are well combined.
5. Pour the batter into the waffle iron and spread it to the edges of the waffle iron to cover all the holes.
6. Close the waffle iron cover and cook for a few minutes, or depending on the waffle iron settings.
7. Once the cooking cycle is complete, remove the waffles from the waffle iron with a silicone or plastic utensil. Follow steps 4-6 until all batter is cooked into the waffles.
8. Garnish each waffle with marinara sauce, finely chopped onion and bell pepper.
9. Cover with mozzarella cheese and place sausage slices on top of cheese filling.
10. Gently place the waffles on the lined baking sheet. Put the tray in the oven, bake for about 5 minutes.
11. Then toast for 1 minute. Take the pizzas out of the oven and let them cook for a few minutes.
12. Serve hot and enjoy!

NUTRITION

Protein 16.8g, Fat 23.2g 30%, Sugars 6.8g, Carbohydrate 14.9g 5%, Calories 350

VANILLA FLAVOURED SOUR CREAM CHAFFLE

INGREDIENTS

- Batter
- 4 eggs
- 1 teaspoon vanilla extract
- 4 ounces sour cream
- ¼ cup stevia
- 1 teaspoon cinnamon
- 5 tablespoons coconut flour
- Other
- 2 tablespoons coconut oil to grease the waffle maker
- ½ teaspoon cinnamon

HOW TO MAKE IT

1. Preheat your waffle maker.
2. Place the eggs and sour cream in a medium bowl, whisk with a fork until smooth.
3. Add the vanilla extract, cinnamon, and stevia and stir together. Add in the coconut flour and stir again.
4. Brush the previously heated waffle maker with some coconut oil and add half of the batter.
5. Close the lid and cook for 7–8 minutes. Allow cooling and top the chaffle with some cinnamon powder per extra flavour. Serve and enjoy.

 COOKING TIME:7—9 MINUTES

NUTRITION

Calories 324, fat 11 g, carbs 8.4 g, sugar 0.5 g, Protein 7.7 g, sodium 77 mg

---

CCC-CHAFFLE (CHOCO CINNAMON COCONUT)

INGREDIENTS

- 2 ground eggs
- 1 tsp. cinnamon powder
- 1/8 cup almond flour
- 1 tsp. sea salt
- 1 cup shredded mozzarella
- 1/2 tsp. baking soda
- Toppings
- 2 tbsps. coconut cream
- 1 tbsp. unsweetened chocolate sauce

HOW TO MAKE IT

1. Preheat a waffle maker and spray it with a non-stick spray.
2. Take a bowl, stir all the cheese and the egg together until smooth.
3. Place half of the batter in the waffle maker, close, and cook for 4 to 5 minutes until golden and crisp.
4. Repeat the process with the remaining mixture. Allow cooling.
5. Coat coconut cream over your chaffles and drizzle chocolate sauce over.
6. Make the chaffles rest in the freezer for about 10 minutes.
7. Remove and enjoy!

 SERVINGS:2

 COOKING TIME:5MINUTES

NUTRITION

Protein: 3, 100 kcal, Fat: 56% Carbohydrates: 5%

PUMPKIN FLAVOURED RICOTTA CHAFFLE

INGREDIENTS

- 1/2 cup ricotta cheese
- 1 tbsp pumpkin puree
- 1 egg, lightly beaten
- 1/4 tsp pumpkin pie spice
- 1 tbsp unsweetened chocolate chips
- 1 tbsp almond flour
- 2 tbsp natural sweetener

HOW TO MAKE IT

1. Preheat your waffle maker and spray waffle iron with cooking spray.
2. In a small bowl, mix egg and pumpkin puree.
3. Add pumpkin pie spice, natural sweetener, almond flour, and cheese and mix well. Stir in chocolate chips.
4. Pour half batter in the hot waffle maker and cook for 4 minutes. Repeat with the remaining batter.
5. Enjoy!

  SERVINGS: 2

COOKING TIME: 15 MINUTES

NUTRITION

Calories 330, Fat 9.2 g Carbohydrates 5.9 g Sugar 0.6 g Protein 6.6 g Cholesterol 70 mg

MAPLE AND ALMOND MILK CHAFFLE

INGREDIENTS

- 2 tbsp. natural sweetener
- 2 egg whites
- 1 egg, lightly beaten
- 1/2 tbsp. baking powder, gluten-free
- 2 tbsp. coconut flour
- 1/2 tbsp. maple extract
- 2 tbsp. almond milk

HOW TO MAKE IT

1. Preheat your waffle iron. In a bowl, beat the egg whites until is whipped. Stir in the maple extract, natural sweetener, baking powder, almond milk, coconut flour and eggs. Spray the waffle iron with cooking spray.
2. Pour half of the batter into the hot waffle iron and bake for 4 minutes or until golden brown.
3. Repeat with the rest of the batter. Serve and enjoy!

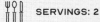 SERVINGS: 2

 COOKING TIME: 15 MINUTES

NUTRITION

Calories 322, Fat 6.6 g, Carbohydrates 9 g, Sugar 1 g, Protein 7 g, Cholesterol 82 mg.

AROMATIC VANILLA AND CINNAMON CHAFFLE

INGREDIENTS

- 1 egg
- 1 tsp baking powder
- ½ cup of mozzarella cheese, shredded
- 1 tsp vanilla
- 1 tsp sweetener
- 2 tbsp almond flour
- 2 tsp cinnamon

HOW TO MAKE IT

1. Preheat your waffle iron, and beat the egg in a bowl.
2. Pour in the rest of the ingredients.
3. Pour half of the batter into the waffle maker. Close it and cook for 4 minutes.
4. Open and place the waffle on a plate.
5. Leave to cool for 2 minutes. Do the same with the rest of the batter.
6. Serve and enjoy!

SERVINGS: 2

COOKING TIME: 8 MINUTES

NUTRITION

Calories 336, Total Fat 7.4g, Saturated Fat 2.9g, Cholesterol 171mg, Potassium 590mg, Sodium 152mg, Dietary Fiber 3.6g, Total Carbohydrate

---

RED VELVET CHAFFLE

INGREDIENTS

- 1 egg,
- ¼ cup mozzarella cheese, shredded
- 1 oz. cream cheese
- 4 tbsp almond flour
- 2 tsp sweetener
- 1 tsp red velvet extract
- 1 tsp baking powder
- 2 tbsp cocoa powder

HOW TO MAKE IT

1. Mix all the ingredients in a bowl.
2. Plug in your waffle iron.
3. Drop some of the batter into the waffle iron.
4. Seal and bake for 5 minutes or until golden bright.
5. Open and transfer to a plate.
6. Now repeat the steps with the rest of the batter.

SERVINGS: 3

COOKING TIME: 12 MINUTES

NUTRITION

Calories 326, Total Fat 10.1g, Saturated Fat 3.4g, Cholesterol 66mg, Potassium 290mg, Sodium 68mg, Dietary Fiber 2.8g, Total Carbohydrate 6.5g, Protein 5.9g, Total Sugars 0.2g.

SWEET WALNUTS CHAFFLES

INGREDIENTS

- 2 tbsps. cream cheese
- 1 large egg
- ¼ cup walnuts, chopped
- Pinch of stevia extract powder
- ¼ tsp baking powder
- ½ tsp almonds flour

HOW TO MAKE IT

I.   Preheat the waffle iron.
2.   Mist the waffle iron with cooking spray. In a bowl, pour cream chee-se, almond flour, egg, walnuts, baking powder, and stevia.
3.   Mix all the ingredients together, pour the nut batter into the waffle iron and cook for about 2-3 minutes.
4.   Leave the waffles to reach room temperature before serving.
5.   Enjoy!

 SERVINGS: 2

 COOKING TIME: 5 MINUTES

NUTRITION

Fat: 80%, Carbohydrates: 8%, Protein: 12%, 323 kcal.

FALL SEASON CHAFFLES

INGREDIENTS

- 2 tsps coconut flour
- 1 tsp baking soda
- 1 cup egg whites
- 1 cup mozzarella cheese, grated
- 1/8 tsp cinnamon powder
- ½ tsp vanilla
- 1 tsp baking powder
- TOPPINGS: keto Chocolate sauce, Cranberries.

HOW TO MAKE IT

I.   Prepare 4 minutes of chaffles with the chaffle ingredients.
2.   Cover with chocolate sauce and cranberry sauce.
3.   Serve hot and taste!

 SERVINGS: 4

 COOKING TIME: 5MINUTES

NUTRITION

389 Kcal, Fat: 57%, Protein: 38% , Carbohydrates: 5%

CHERRY WHIPPING CREAM CHAFFLE

INGREDIENTS

- 2 tbsp sugar-free cherry pie filling
- 1 egg, lightly beaten
- 1/2 tsp baking powder, gluten-free
- 1 tbsp unsweetened chocolate chips
- 1/2 cup mozzarella cheese, shredded
- 1 tbsp natural sweetener
- 2 tbsp heavy whipping cream
- 1 tbsp almond flour
- 1 tbsp unsweetened cocoa powder

HOW TO MAKE IT

1. Preheat the waffle iron. In a bowl, whisk together the egg, cheese, baking powder, natural sweetener, cocoa powder and almond flour.
2. Mist the waffle iron with cooking spray.
3. Place the batter in the hot waffle iron and cook until golden brown.
4. Cover with the cherry pie filling, whipped cream and chocolate shavings.
5. Serve and enjoy!

 SERVINGS: 2

 COOKING TIME: 5 MINUTES

NUTRITION

Calories 370, Carbohydrates 8.5 g, Fat 22 g, Protein 12.7 g, Sugar 0.5 g, Cholesterol 212 mg.

- -

SALMON, EGG & AVOCADO CHAFFLE

INGREDIENTS

- 2 eggs
- Cooking spray
- 2 leaves lettuce
- 4 slices Smoked Salmon
- 4 basic chaffles
- ½ avocado, mashed

NUTRITION

Calories 372, Total Fat 30.1g, Saturated Fat 8.6g, Cholesterol 205mg, Total Carbohydrate 5.4g

HOW TO MAKE IT

1. Cover skillet with cooking spray. Stir fry capocollo slices until golden brown and crispy. Move to a plate lined with paper towels.
2. Break eggs into the same skillet and cook until firm. Turn and cook until the yolk is set.
3. Sprinkle avocado on top of the taffeta.
4. Top with lettuce, egg and Smoked Salmon.
5. Finish with another chaffle.
6. Serve and enjoy!

 SERVINGS: 2

 COOKING TIME: 5 MINUTES

CRUNCHY BANANA AND WALNUT CHAFFLES

INGREDIENTS

- 4 tbsp. almond flour
- 1 egg
- 2 tbsp. sweetener
- 1 oz. cream cheese
- 2 tbsp. walnuts, chopped
- 1 tbsp. baking powder
- ¼ cup mozzarella cheese, shredded
- 1 tsp. banana extract

HOW TO MAKE IT

1. Mix all the ingredients in a bowl. Switch on the waffle iron. Add the batter to the waffle iron.
2. Shut and cook for a few minutes. Open and put the waffle to a plate.
3. Cool it for 2 minutes.
4. Do the same steps with the remaining batter.
5. Serve and enjoy!

SERVINGS: 2

COOKING TIME: 5 MINUTES

NUTRITION

Calories 269, Total Fat 14g, Cholesterol 99mg, Saturated Fat 4.6g, Sodium 98mg, Dietary Fiber 2g, Potassium 343mg, Protein 5g, Total Sugars 0.6g, Total Carbohydrate 5.6g

- -

CHOCOLATE CINNAMON ROLL CHAFFLES

INGREDIENTS

- 2 tbsp peanut oil for topping
- 1 tbsp almond flour
- 1 large egg
- ½ tsp baking powder
- 1 tbsp cocoa powder
- 1 tsp cinnamon powder
- 1/2 cup cheddar chees.

HOW TO MAKE IT

1. Prepare the waffle iron and mix all the ingredients together. Place the waffle mixture in the center of the oiled waffle iron.
2. Shut the waffle iron.
3. Cook the chaffle for about 5 minutes until cooked and crispy.
4. When the waffles are cooked, remove them.
5. Stir the melted butter oil over the top.
6. Serve and enjoy!

SERVINGS: 2

COOKING TIME: 5 MINUTES

NUTRITION

Protein: 15%, Fat: %, Carbohydrates: 3%, 247 kcal

MEASUREMENTS & CONVERSIONS

3 teaspoons	1 tablespoon
2 tablespoons	1 ounce
4 tablespoons	¼ cup
8 tablespoons	½ cup
16 tablespoons	1 cup
2 cups	1 pint
4 cups	1 quart
4 quarts	1 gallon

Type	Imperial	Imperial	Metric
Weight	1 dry ounce		28g
	1 pound	16 dry ounces	0.45 kg
Volume	1 teaspoon		5 ml
	1 dessert spoon	2 teaspoons	10 ml
	1 tablespoon	3 teaspoons	15 ml
	1 Australian tablespoon	4 teaspoons	20 ml
	1 fluid ounce	2 tablespoons	30 ml
	1 cup	16 tablespoons	240 ml
	1 cup	8 fluid ounces	240 ml
	1 pint	2 cups	470 ml
	1 quart	2 pints	0.95 l
	1 gallon	4 quarts	3.8 l
Length	1 inch		2.54 cm

* Numbers are rounded to the closest equivalent

Gluten-Free – Conversion Tables

All pourpose flour	Rice Flour	Potato Starch	Tapioca	Xanthan Gum
½ cup	1/3 cup	2 tablespoons	1 tablespoon	¼ teaspoon
1 cup	½ cup	3 tablespoons	1 tablespoon	½ teaspoon
¼ cup	¾ cup	1/3 cup	3 tablespoons	2/3 teaspoon
1 ½ cup	1 cup	5 tablespoons	3 tablespoons	2/3 teaspoon
1 ¾ cup	1 ¼ cup	5 tablespoons	3 tablespoons	1 teaspoon
2 cups	1 ½ cup	1/3 cup	1/3 cup	1 teaspoon
2 ½ cups	1 ½ cup	½ cup	¼ cup	1 1/8 teaspoon
2 2/3 cups	2 cups	½ cup	¼ cup	1 ¼ teaspoon
3 cups	2 cups	2/3 cup	1/3 cup	1 ½ cup

Flour: quantity and weight

1 cup = 140 grams
3/4 cup = 105 grams
1/2 cup = 70 grams
1/4 cup = 35 grams

Sugar: quantity and weight

1 cup = 200 grams
3/4 cup = 150 grams
2/3 cup = 135 grams
1/2 cup = 100 grams
1/3 cup = 70 grams
1/4 cup = 50 grams

Powdered Sugar

1 cup = 160 grams
3/4 cup = 120 grams
1/2 cup = 80 grams
1/4 cup = 40 grams

Cream: quantity and weight

1 cup = 250 ml = 235 grams
3/4 cup = 188 ml = 175 grams
1/2 cup = 125 ml = 115 grams
1/4 cup = 63 ml = 60 grams
1 tablespoon = 15 ml = 15 grams

Oven Temperature Equivalent Chart

°F	°C	Gas Mark
220	100	
225	110	1/4
250	120	1/2
275	140	1
300	150	2
325	160	3
350	180	4
375	190	5
400	200	6
425	220	7
450	230	8
475	250	9
500	260	

Butter: quantity and weight

1 cup = 8 ounces = 2 sticks = 16 tablespoons =230 grams
1/2 cup = 4 ounces = 1 stick = 8 tablespoons = 115 grams
¼ cup = 2 ounces = ½ stick = 4 tablespoons= 58 grams

CONCLUSION

I am sure by now you have fallen in love with chaffles.

The irresistible ketogenic waffle that can make your Keto diet easier and more enjoyable. Now that you've tried how versatile and how good they taste, I hope they will be present in many of your breakfasts, lunches, dinners and snacks! They are a constant presence in my diet, and the've been a big time-saver when my schedule in the bakery has been too busy to sustain a more relaxed dinner. That's why everybody is joining in this new successful trend, which, as the best inventions in kitchen's history, it is meant stay.

Enjoy your new way to eat; enjoy your stay in Chaffle World!

With love,

Camilla

AND IF YOU HAVE ENJOYED THIS BOOK, CHECK OUT ALSO MY OTHER BOOK ON HOW TO MAKE DELICIOUS AND PERFECT HOME-MADE BREAD IN NO TIME WITH A BREAD MACHINE!

THE MODERN

BREAD MACHINE COOKBOOK

SIMPLE HANDS-OFF RECIPES TO MAKE PERFECT HOMEMADE BREAD WITH ANY BREAD MAKER

INCLUDES GLUTEN-FREE RECIPES

100+ PICTURES

PHOEBE COLLINS

INDEX

Made in United States
Troutdale, OR
12/04/2024

25873373R00055